THE
DREAMLAND COMPANION

THE DREAMLAND COMPANION

A Bedside Diary and Guide to
Dream Interpretation

by Ilan Kutz, M.D.

HYPERION

NEW YORK

Acknowledgments

For her devotion and readiness to do whatever needed to be done in order to make this project possible, I thank my wife, Sue.

For helping me to broaden and deepen my understanding of the human brain, the psyche, and dreams, I thank J. Allan Hobson and Devorah Kutzinsky.

For help with early design ideas, I thank Menachem Regev, Ami Shavit, and Tina Silverman, and for generous contribution of their art work, I thank Yosl Bergner and Luis Azaceta.

For her help, I also thank Esther Dinur at Mishkenot Shaananim.

Illustrations in this work appear with the permission of the following:
"The Scarecrow," Erwin Shenkelbach, Jerusalem. "Horus Papyrus," Ancient Art and Architecture Collection, London. "The Sleep of Reason Begets Monsters," Francisco José de Goya. Philadelphia Museum of Art. "The Caress," Fernand Khnopff. Musées royaux des Beaux-Arts de Belgique, Brussels. "Night," Ferdinand Hodler. Kunstmuseum Bern, Staat Bern. "The Labyrinth," Robert Vickrey. Collection of Whitney Museum of American Art. "La Reproduction Interdite," René Magritte. Museum Boymans-van Beuningen, Rotterdam. "The Secret," by Erwin Shenkelbach, Jerusalem. "Black Night's Move," Ilan Kutz, Tel Aviv. "Jacob Wrestling with an Angel," Rembrandt. Gemaldegalerie Staatliche Museen PreuBischer Kulturbesitz, Berlin. "The Prayer of Jacob," Gustav Doré. Dover Publications, New York. "Jacob Wrestling with the Angel," Gustav Doré. Dover Publications, New York. "The Meeting of Jacob and Esau," Gustav Doré. Dover Publications, New York. "The Reflection," Kinuko Y. Craft. © 1985 Kinuko Y. Craft. "The Dream of the Blessed Virgin," Simone dei Crocifissi. Pinacoteca, Ferrara. "The Butterfly Eaters," Yosl Bergner. Yosl Bergner, Tel Aviv. "Couple with Their Heads Full of Clouds," Salvador Dali. Museum Boymans-van Beuningen, Rotterdam. "The Crow People," Anonymous. "Tea Cup in a Tempest," Ilan Kutz, Tel Aviv, Israel. "Jerusalem Ghost," Erwin Shenkelbach, Jerusalem. "Punishment of Luxury," Giovanni Segantini. Walker Art Gallery, Liverpool. "The Island of the Dead," Arnold Böcklin. Colorphoto Hans Hinz, Basel. "In the Fourth Dimension," Erwin Shenkelbach, Jerusalem. "Return from the Fourth Dimension," Erwin Shenkelbach, Jerusalem. "Entering the Fourth Dimension," Erwin Shenkelbach, Jerusalem. "The Way of Silence," František Kupka. Narodni Gelerie v Praze, Prague. "Le Domaine D'Arnheim," René Magritte. © ADAGP, Paris 1992. "Alice in Wonderland, Backup," John Tenniel. "Alice in Wonderland, the Caterpillar," John Tenniel. "Nightmare," Darryl Zudeck, New York. "The Fairy Feller's Master Stroke," Richard Dadd. Tate Gallery, London/Art Resource, New York. "The Puzzle," Ilan Kutz, Tel Aviv. "Return of the Wooden Horse," Yosl Bergner, Tel Aviv. "The House of Glass," René Magritte. Museum Boymans-van Beuningen, Rotterdam. "Soul Love," Jean Delville. Musée d'Ixelles, Brussels. "War Head: Dangerous Dream," Luis Cruz Azaceta, New York. "The Lay of the Land," Jerry LoFaro, New York. "Job and His Friends," Gustav Doré. Dover Publications, New York. "Study from the Human Body," Francis Bacon. National Gallery of Victoria, Melbourne. "Nightbird," Ilan Kutz, Tel Aviv. "La Condition Humaine," René Magritte. National Gallery of Art, Washington, D.C. "Jacob's Ladder" from Lambeth Bible. Lambeth Palace Library. "Joseph Interpreting Pharaoh's Dream," Gustav Doré. Dover Publications. "The Wounded Angel," Hugo Simberg. The Central Archives, Helsinki. "The Red Tower," Giorgio De Chirico. © 1991 The Solomon R. Guggenheim Foundation. "The Alarm," Yosl Bergner, Tel Aviv. "Deluge," Albrecht Dürer. Kunsthistorisches Museum, Vienna. "The Closet Girl," Yosl Bergner, Tel Aviv. "La Charmeuse de Serpents," Henri Rousseau. Musée d'Orsay, Paris.

Library of Congress Cataloging-in-Publication Data
Kutz, Ilan.
    The dreamland companion : a diary and guide to dream
interpretation / by Ilan Kutz.—1st ed.
      p. cm.
    ISBN 1-56282-935-1
    1. Dreams. I. Title.
    BF1078.K88 1993
    154.6'3—dc20
                                            92-23343
                                          CIP

FIRST EDITION
10 9 8 7 6 5 4 3 2 1

Cover design: Carin Goldberg
Cover painting: Arnold Böcklin, *Island of the Dead;* The Metropolitan Museum of Art, Reisinger Fund, 1926.

To all those who share their dreams in the quest for self-knowledge

Erwin Shenkelbach (1930–   )
The Scarecrow   **Though meant to scare the birds, this Jerusalem scarecrow reminds us of the shadow of our fears.**

Contents

Preface: Invitation to Dreamland

We are such stuff
As dreams are made on . . .

Shakespeare

You journey to the strange land of dreams every night. The wondrous, bizarre impressions you bring back are coded messages that, when interpreted, delineate the contours of your inner landscape. *The Dreamland Companion* is a travel logbook that will help you preserve the memory of these discoveries and a guidebook that will lead you to their hidden meanings.

This is a book for the curious, for those who wish to tap the workings of the mind and explore hidden information that may not be available otherwise. There is no more danger in probing one's dreams than in entering a hall of mirrors, for a dream is but a distorted reflection of the self that will remain merely funny or frightening until one is ready to see beyond the overt, warped image. Even though these reflected images may sometimes seem unflattering, to look at the unadorned picture of the inner self can be very rewarding, since to know split-off "other sides" of the self is to have the opportunity to integrate them and thereby feel whole.

The process of decoding and interpreting the message of dreams is known as "dream work," and there is little work in one's life with half as much fun and excitement as playing around with what is a cross between exotic travel and puzzle-solving. Beyond the fun is the discovery that the puzzle's picture you try to complete is the portrait of your very self.

The Dreamland Companion offers memory-enhancing tips and suggests special layouts to make decoding your dreams easier. Once your interpretive skills have improved, you can retrieve and reexamine any particular dream, and uncover repeated themes and recurring patterns in a series of dreams with the aid of the Calendar-Index section. When you get stuck, as you invariably will, *The Dreamland Companion* will show you how to become unstuck, when possible, and when and how to turn to others for feedback and help.

The Dreamland Companion is based on the proven psychological premise that only the dreamer holds the clues to the symbols and riddles that appear in his/her dreams. What is taught are not readymade answers, but rather the various ways to ask the right questions. All you have to do is start asking.

FROM THE GODS TO THE SELF: A HISTORY OF DREAM INTERPRETATION

Know Thyself

—The dictum inscribed at the Temple of the Oracle at Delphi

Divine History

Throughout the ages, dreams have been thought to be not only internal visions, but also visitations of external deities or guiding forces of fate—predicting, heralding, instructing, warning, or bringing cure. This may have been believed in prehistoric times, and it has been documented as early as the year 5000 B.C. by the Babylonians and Assyrians, who compiled an impressive literature on dreams, including elaborate instructions for dream interpretation. Similarly, the ancient Egyptians regarded dream interpretation seriously, attributing cures to the dream gods Serapis, Bes, and Horus.

The Horus Papyrus **One of the most ancient texts on dreams known, written by the priests of the Egyptian god Horus some four thousand years ago.**

The Hellenic era saw the flourishing of the cult of dream incubation, in which people slept and dreamt in sacred dream temples in order to have their dreams interpreted by expert dream priests. By the second century A.D. several hundred dream temples of Aesculapius, the god of medicine and healing, were spread throughout the Greek and Roman empires.

Dreams could "divinely" determine individual decisions, and, if the individuals were influential, their dreams could change the fates of nations. The Old Testament is abundant with examples of important dreamers and their dreams. Jacob's famous dream of angels walking up and down a ladder is seen as the sign of a divine promise of the land of Canaan for him and his seed. Joseph, Jacob's son, is first led into slavery and then elevated to princely power in the court of Pharaoh, because of his exceptional powers as a dreamer and dream interpreter. His dreams alter the course of events of the Egyptian empire, as well as that of his people, the Israelites. So important were dreams in ancient times that lack of dreams at crucial moments was felt to be disastrous. Tragic King Saul, on the eve of his fatal battle with the Philistines, desperately seeks the help of a spirit-raising witch (the kind of soothsayer he had earlier persecuted and banished), because "God answers me no more . . . by dreams." (I Samuel 28:15) In the New Testament, Christ and Christianity appear in a dream of Joseph and dreams later play a part in Christian lore.

Central to the Muslim Koran are the dreams of Muhammad and some of his followers.

"The Royal Road to the Unconscious": Freud, Jung, and Modern Psychology
In addition to their spiritual resonance, dreams have provoked scientific curiosity throughout history. Greek philosophers such as Aristotle, and physicians such as Hippocrates, regarded dreams as natural "movements" of the mind-body. Artemidorus of Daldis, a second-century Greek philosopher and dream scholar, composed a five-volume book, *Oneirocritica* ("Interpretation of Dreams"), in which several thousand dreams are chronicled and followed by instructions for interpretation.

The interpretations of these scholars contain some striking insights that are consistent with modern scientific thinking, such as the notion of coincidence rather than prophecy; the need to know the dreamer's cultural background in order to better understand the dream's symbols; the dream's ability to pick up subtle bodily changes, including early signs of disease; the fact that some dreams are not symbolic, requiring deciphering, but are concrete, reflecting mundane experience; the need to scan some series of dreams as though they were one, in order to understand their meaning, and the usefulness of incubation techniques, which enable us to induce dreams by suggestion.

Despite these ancient innovative observations it was not until the year 1900, when Sigmund Freud published *The Interpretation of Dreams,* that a massive change in viewing dreams occurred, influencing the twentieth-century worlds of psychology, art, and science. Although many of Freud's first ideas about the origin and function of dreams have been modified, altered, or even proved outright wrong, it was he, in calling dreams "the royal road to the unconscious," who was responsible for shifting the meaning of dreams from the sphere of the divine to the internal, psychological realm. "The technique which I describe . . . differs in one essential respect from the ancient method: it imposes the task of interpretation upon the dreamer himself." This was a revolutionary change in emphasis. What had been regarded largely as supernatural forces from beyond became principal reflections of the structure and struggles within.

Freud correctly identified the mechanisms operating during the dream, and originated the ingenious method of "free association" to the details in the dream. Current thinking is, however, that Freud's original dream theory over-emphasized prohibited wishes, most notably forbidden sexual themes.

Carl Gustav Jung, though accepting Freud's basic formulations about the structure and language of dreams, and about the method of interpretation through associations, regarded dreams as reflecting not simply past conflicts, from which the dreamer needed to be defended, but messages with a current purpose: the dreamer is aspiring toward growth and individuation. Linking his study of dream symbols with those symbols used in primitive societies, Jung also expanded the meaning of the dream from the strictly personal to the universal, claiming that there was ". . . an inborn disposition to produce . . . identical psychic structures common to all men, which I later called the archetypes of the collective unconscious." According to Jungian theory, primary experiences such as birth, death, love, hate, sex, parenting, and so on, are expressed as symbols, identical in both dreams and the myths of all cultures.

If Freud seemed to be saying, "Show me your dreams and I'll show you the origins of your disturbance," Jung was implying, "Show me your dreams and I'll show you what you are striving to achieve, and what stands in the way." No wonder Jung's theories found more followers in those spiritually or mystically inclined. Whatever the historical differences between these schools, Freud's and Jung's modern enlightened disciples seem to be more alike than different in their approach to dream interpretation, stressing the existence and importance of the unconscious aspects of the mind and regarding the visions of the night as conveyors of messages from within. Both schools share the conviction that to understand one's dream is to be in better communication with one's self.

The Dreaming Brain

The entire field of sleep and dream research took a giant step forward in 1953, when two American scientists, Eugene Aserinsky and Nathaniel Kleitman, began to record electrical brain activity during sleep. They discovered that during certain periods of sleep the slow-wave activity of the sleeping brain suddenly shifts pattern, displaying rapid shallow waves for extended periods of time, as if the brain were wide awake. They called this phase Rapid Eye Movement sleep (or REM sleep), because of the relatively fast left-right movement of the eyes under the closed eyelids during this period. Curiously enough, the rapid eye movement and the accompanying increase in pulse and respiratory rate are the only physical indications of the brain's robust activity, while the rest of the body is virtually immobilized, and no movements of tossing or turning occur at this stage. The researchers further discovered that these REM periods correspond to dreaming activity.

With the discovery of REM, sleep was suddenly recognized as a complex state, with its own "architecture" of predictable electrical patterns, which are of two major distinct kinds: REM and non-REM sleep. Non-REM sleep is comprised of four stages of gradual depth change: from the awake state to Stage I sleep, or dozing, through the light sleep of Stage II to the deeper sleep of Stages III and IV. Accordingly, the brain's electrical waves become slower and larger, displaying the typical spindle waves of sleep.

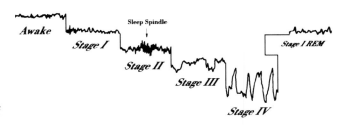

Stages of Sleep **This diagram illustrates the first sleep cycle of the night.**

It is during the REM activity of the brain that most dreaming occurs. If people are awakened while their brains display the typical electrical REM wave pattern, four out of five times they will report an interrupted dream. In fact, this is the basis of the technique of modern dream lab research. The scientist waits for the typical rapid-shallow waves of the REM state to appear on the monitor, then wakes the subject and asks for a dream report. Dreams appear also in the non-REM state, but they are much rarer. Only one out of ten awakened sleepers will report a dream in the non-REM state, and the dream is likely to be shorter, less vivid, less bizarre, and less elaborate than the REM-sleep dreams.

REM waves are initiated in a specialized group of cells in the more "primitive" part of the brain, at the top of the spinal cord, called the brainstem. From there they travel via neural pathways, to the posterior cortex, the higher part of the brain responsible for the processing of visual imagery usually coming from the eyes. The arriving REM waves "excite" the visual processing center and adjacent associative areas, and rekindle recent images and memory associations to them. This neural wiring explains why dreams are mainly pictorial in nature, and why recent events are almost always present as a "day residue" part of dreams. Other REM waves travel to motoric centers and activate them causing, together with the visual excitation, the sensation of motion. That may explain why walking, running and falling are so common in dreams. The reason that we do not get up and run during dreaming is because at the same time another neural circuit connects to the motoric center in the brain and paralyzes the bodily muscles except those of the eyes and the face.

During the night's sleep, REM and non-REM states alternate in cycles. The amount of time spent in each of these stages varies with age, REM sleep being highest in infancy and childhood and decreasing with age. In adults, the REM sleep state begins, on an average night, about one hour after the onset of the four-staged non-REM sleep, and lasts only a few minutes at the beginning of the night. As the night proceeds, the non-REM sleep cycles become shorter and shallower, consisting mostly of Stage II, or light sleep, while the REM periods, appearing every ninety minutes on average, become longer, up to forty-five minutes toward morning. Hence, most dreams, certainly most remembered dreams, occur in the early morning hours, when both dreaming intensity and the chances of waking to remember these dreams are highest. The REM state can also appear during short naps and brief dozes. At those times, the "REM latency," or the time elapsed from the beginning of sleep until the first REM bout, may be shorter, appearing minutes or even seconds after falling asleep.

On an ordinary night, we spend an average of an hour and a half to two hours dreaming away. If we take into account that during infancy and childhood considerably more time is spent in REM sleep, one could calculate that several years of one's lifetime are spent in the dreaming state. REM activity is vital for harmonious mental functioning, and if not enough time is spent in a REM state, after several nights a "REM debt" develops, which manifests itself in various impairments of awake mental functioning. When normal sleep is resumed, the debt is paid by longer and more intense REM bouts.

The awake state and REM sleep, despite similar electrical brain-wave patterns, are diametrically opposed in their chemical, behavioral, and mental aspects. The sleep and awake states are generated in different parts of the brain. The chemical equilibrium that controls the awake state is the reverse of the one that controls the REM stage. The voluntary motor activity of the awake state is in contrast to the complete paralysis (except for eye movements) of the REM state. Finally, each state processes information very differently. The awake information processing is constantly "fed" by external clues. It operates according to the laws of accepted reason, where one fact or idea leads to a logical other, allowing for organization of a massive amount of the incoming data. The REM activity, on the other hand, emanates almost exclusively from an internal brain source, being relatively insensitive to input from external reality. This REM mental activity seems, to the awake mind, bizarre and discontinuous, illogical and erratic. REM mental processing is worthless for the organization and storage of data. REM material is not stored in memory, and rapidly evaporates unless it is transferred to awake awareness.

Memory Span of Dreams
Contrary to certain psychoanalytical thought, the rapid forgetting of one's dreams is largely a product of physiology and not psyche. Psychoanalysts have believed that forgetfulness of a dream's content is a sign of "censorship" by the unconscious, an active repression of the dream's "risky" content. In fact, the situation may be quite the reverse. Meaningful dreams, those that profoundly

move us, tend to linger much longer, sometimes for an entire lifetime, or to repeat themselves, precisely because they carry such loaded meaning, whereas emotionally indifferent dreams tend to be wiped off the mental slate, as they are felt to be of no interest. The emotionally stirring dreams are also the ones that tell us most about our inner world. However evocative, emotionally significant dreams are the minority compared to the constantly produced and forgotten "nonsense" dream images manufactured at every REM corner, several times a night.

According to dream physiology, the freshly awakened brain forgets dreams because it is still under the influence of the neurotransmitter system (the acetylcholine system) that operates during sleep and inhibits memory. Memory physiology may also explain why telling the dream content to someone, or writing it on a piece of paper, enables one to capture it in memory. During the awake activities of talking or writing, the brain switches gears to the opposing transmitter system (dominated by the noradrenergic and serotonergic systems), which enhances the preservation of memory. Thus, the activity of writing or talking one's dream not only secures a witness to its content but also shifts the brain into a better mode for remembering it.

Dreams as Statements of the Self
Despite scientific discoveries that explain how we sleep and dream, research has not come up with a conclusive theory that explains why we dream. There are clearly biological reasons for REM sleep, to which the REM sleep of mammals and the almost continuous REM sleep of fetuses, as well as the consequences of REM deprivation, attest. In addition, the personal and universal experience of dreaming supports the notion of an essential, psychological function to dreaming, complementing the psychological mental functions of the awake state. And although sleep researchers explain many of the dream's characteristics, such as bizarreness and discontinuity, as a natural property of the brain's unique physiology during REM sleep, they do not deny the psychological premise that the dreaming brain can evoke original reformulations and syntheses of central psychological dilemmas, in a fashion less available to the "organized" waking state. In fact, some researchers claim that for both animals and humans dreams consolidate information with survival value. For humans the foundations of im-

portant and intense experiences lie in early life. It is therefore not surprising that dreams of adults include fragments of childhood memories as recurring background in dreams.

Any internal state is comprised of what is conscious and what is unconscious. By definition, the unconscious constitutes those emotions and attitudes of which we are not aware. It is a necessary part of the human psyche, the storage place for those feelings and ideas that may get in the way while we are going about our daily routine. It is also the place to which conflict-causing, painful, or unpleasant emotions are diverted, where they may reside outside of awareness for short or lengthy periods of time, depending on how ready we are to accept them. As new data keep pouring in, this unconscious part of mental life demands, just as does its conscious counterpart, updating, rearranging, and integration, even if this updating proceeds outside of awareness.

It is tempting to assume that the dreaming mode of the brain provides some opportunity for the processing of conscious and unconscious information, matching unconscious data with recently acquired conscious feelings and facts, integrating the known and unknown. In other words, there is a kind of nocturnal review process in which new data is compared and confronted with the old, in an attempt to resolve emotional discrepancies and conflicts and to give priority to psychic material according to its personal emotional relevance. The dream is the reflection of that reviewing activity on the mind's screen. If there are difficulties in integration, as in times of conflict and crisis, dreams are likely to reflect this internal clash. If integration succeeds, the person wakens clear of mind, with a solution or resolution to what has been so vexing just a few hours before. The commonsense expression "go sleep on it" comes from this organizing, integrative capacity of sleep and dreams. Thus, examining one's dream provides a unique glimpse into the hidden works of the mind, an opportunity to receive, albeit in code, the transcripts of the ongoing dialogues between parts of the inner self.

The following example illustrates how a dream can provide essential, otherwise unavailable, information about the self.

Joining the French Foreign Legion

Background: A group of people, who had never met one another before, were having a tea-time social conversation about dreams with the author. A retired professor and man of letters half-mockingly challenged the notion of dream interpretation: "If dreams make any sense," he defied the author, "then tell me why I dreamt the other night that, of all things, I was joining the French Foreign Legion. Of all the armies in the world, I detest it the most. It is an abhorrent organization, one that takes recruits of all nationalities, robs them of their names and identities, making them all the same in the service of an evil force. Once you have joined, you can't leave." When asked if he really wanted to know what the dream meant, he willingly went on to recount the entire dream.

The dream: I am standing in a line of new recruits in front of a French Foreign Legion recruitment post, a kind of a tent, somewhere in a desolate desert. As they keep moving along into the tent, one by one, I keep retreating, trying to stay at the end of the line, but knowing that my time will come soon. I keep wondering how I came to be there. Suddenly, I see a very good friend Albert (He is French. Incidentally, he died only some months ago) in the uniform of a French Foreign Legion soldier. I say to him, "Albert, what are *you* doing here? He looks at me and gives one of his famous, wide-open-arms shrugs, which expresses puzzlement, bewilderment and helplessness.

The dream work: At that point, the wife of the dreamer said: "I believe I understand the meaning of your dream." So did many of the other listeners. When invited by him, she said: "When you mentioned Albert, our French friend, it became clear to me that you are afraid of dying, like he." Then the author added that the dreamer's descriptions of the abhorred French Foreign Legion, which "robs the name and identity, and signs one up forever," symbolizes death, which he feels is an eternal loss of identity. When the dreamer heard all this, he immediately protested, "But curiously enough, I don't feel I am afraid of dying. Let death come; I am ready any day!" It was then suggested to him that that is what he consciously feels, and that his dream was telling him that unconsciously he feels very differently. He became silent, clearly moved, and then said, "I guess you have a point. It is something to think about."

Risks and Benefits of Dream Interpretation

The condensed images of the dream—the sum of innocuous events, overt and covert wishes and worries, current and ancient premonitions and longings, all thrown and held together by loosely associated metaphors and symbols—contain the code to one's emotional workings. The dreamer of the French Foreign

Legion obviously had been preoccupied with his dream, so much so that he initiated the public challenge and volunteered to unfold his dream's details in public. It was also plain that his ignorance of the dream's message was not a result of the complexity of the dream's symbols but rather a defense mechanism. All those present in the room, aside from him, could intuit what the dream meant. This demonstrates that the supposed "defensive function" is fulfilled not by the dream's plot but by the waking defenses, which resist the almost obvious meanings. Although initially the dreamer's conscious defenses were making one last stand against admitting the dreaded feeling of the fear of death, once that fear was revealed and understood he was clearly relieved. To be in touch with all sides of one's true feelings, even negative ones, is usually to feel relief, in contrast to the tension felt as a result of rigidly maintaining a split-off, double emotional bookkeeping.

But is it really safe to decipher hidden aspects of one's self, "to be in touch" with one's inner feelings? Is it not better to "let sleeping dreams lie"? Perhaps the release of these forbidden, painful, or frightening feelings can be dangerous to one's mental health, and their suppression is important. Perhaps, in other words, the unconscious is not conscious for good reason.

José de Francisco Goya y Lucientes (1746–1828), *Sleep of Reason Begets Monsters* **The fear of the unknown forces that may be unleashed in sleep is illustrated by Goya, a painter of genius, who was given to depressive periods and haunting visions.**

There is some validity to the fear that some feelings, or intensity of feeling, can be overwhelming. That is why we deploy defenses, like denial and repression, which enable the psyche to "not see," or, in other words, to make unconscious what it can't handle. Such defense mechanisms are essential for functioning in a crisis, and are necessary to some extent all of the time.

Defenses, however, can be costly. They are difficult to regulate and, like the brooms of the sorcerer's apprentice, can keep on operating long after there is a need for them. After a while, it is the ongoing defensiveness, in the form of neurotic behavior and physical symptoms, which has become the problem. The maintenance of a defense system consumes a great deal of mental effort. It inhibits fluid functioning, sometimes to the point of depression. Thus, while some constant repression is necessary, that which is unnecessary must be lifted, so that vital mental energy is freed. The feelings of the unconscious tend to assume their most fearful proportions simply because they are confined. When set loose, they tend to assume everyday dimensions, and can be better handled. But wakefulness, the faithful servant of reason, won't let go of its defenses so easily. One must wait for the reasoning mind to sleep in order to let such feelings loose.

The natural properties of the dreaming brain, i.e., the absence of memory function during sleep and the condensed symbols of the dream that create a puzzling code, unite together to form an excellent safety valve. That we do not remember most dreams is probably the most common and surest way of avoiding, while awake, mentally threatening "dream stuff." As for those dreams that have managed to cross the sleep barrier into waking memory but contain information that is too "risky," they will not be understood by the dreamer once he is awake. He/she will disregard with vehemence or indifference any interpretation of the plot or symbols for which he is unready. He/she will use other defenses, notably rationalization, to explain away unwanted conclusions, and will not interpret correctly a dream whose message he/she isn't ready to handle. Only when the dreamer is ready to tap deep-seated emotions and expose hidden premonitions and passions, will he/she do so.

At times, dreams can serve as guides to decision-making and problem-solving. In periods of great conflict, personal stress, or social distress, people are likely to produce dreams in abundance, many of which seem premonitory or oracular, as if a window had been opened into the future. Such a feeling of clairvoyance is what endowed dreams throughout the ages with their special position as heralds of events to come. Dreams cannot be oracles in the sense of predicting or determining future events, but they can resonate with the voice of the authentic self, that inner voice that says what is "right for you," a voice that is always useful to heed when attempting to make a crucial personal decision. At such times of crisis and crippling doubt, dreams can be "incubated," that is specifically summoned by conscious suggestion, so that we can make use of their reflection of inner knowledge, hopes, and fears to enable us to make "educated" guesses about what will or should happen. When a deadline is near, but the emotions aren't, when obsessive rational arguments "for and against" confound the issue at hand, mobilizing the reliable inner voice via an "oracle dream" can be dramatically effective in providing a guiding answer.

The Star, the Winged Horse, and the Crawling Bread

Background: One pregnant woman, whose fetus was at risk for the same "short-limb" congenital deformity from which she herself suffered, couldn't make up her mind whether or not to abort her pregnancy. As the deadline for her decision was drawing near, she was driving herself and others crazy with her lists of rational "for and against" arguments. She was "ordered" by her physician to stop her obsessive consultations and try to see if she could come up with an inner conviction in the form of a dream.

The dream: I see a young woman standing at the edge of a high cliff in front of an abyss. It is nighttime. Suddenly some bright stars appear in the sky, one of them shining brilliantly in the heavens before me, something like a comet. Then there appears a winged horse, and she mounts it. As they are soaring upward, the woman and horse unify into one creature, half woman, half winged horse, as in the ancient Greek legends, and they keep soaring up. Then the woman is riding the horse again, this time in the desert. She is holding a bag, with a loaf of bread in it. She hurls the bag far away. The bag falls on the sands, and the loaf rolls out of the bag. Then the loaf of bread grows a head and short limbs, and begins to crawl.

The dream work: The woman on the cliff is her self, facing the abyss of indecision. *The bright star*, like those common in history and folklore, is a symbol for someone important about to be born. *The Winged Horse* was, for her, a sense of new horizons, and *the merging and soaring* with the horse, forming a chimera, was "as if something was merging with me," the joy of the forming baby within her and becoming a new being herself, a mother. *The desert scene* captured the feeling of aloneness and desolation that she had been experiencing in the past few months when her marriage was breaking up and she had felt all alone with the pregnancy and conflict. *The loaf of bread* was, for her, "something sacred, something essential which shouldn't be discarded." *The bag* holding the bread was "a weak bag, the kind that was already torn once and was bound to tear again," an allusion to a previous pregnancy that was terminated by a spontaneous abortion, making her realize that the bag was her uterus. *The bread growing head and short limbs and crawling around* represented her fear of having a baby with short-limb syndrome, as well as the unavoidable fact that the baby was destined to live.

This elaborate, archetypal night vision, full of mythological symbols, portrayed both the dreamer's fear and her previously unrecognized determination to go ahead with her pregnancy. It is important to notice that without aid, in this case the "expert other," who can help summon a dream by suggestion, and then assist in interpreting the "oracle dream," the chances of benefiting from this "incubation technique" are small. Also, if one is not ready to make a critical life decision, the summoned dream may simply reflect that unreadiness rather than provide a solution.

While great conflict can produce "oracular dreams" with archetypal or dramatic symbols, dreams can also serve as guides even in mundane concerns. Here is an example:

> ### The Double Date
> *Background:* The dreamer is a young woman, who returns from a blind date. The man had seemed pleasant, considerate, and very attractive; he is anxious to meet with her again. Once at home, she tries to make sense of a gnawing uneasiness, but fails to understand what is wrong, since the date had appeared to be a start to a possibly wonderful relationship. She goes to sleep.
> *The dream:* In her dream, her date of the previous evening appears at the door holding flowers, but he is simultaneously her date and her ex-husband.
> *The dream work:* She wakes up, stirred and intrigued. Through associative dream work, she recognizes that the cruel, sadistic streak of her ex-husband, well hidden behind a soft-spoken, polished façade, may be shared by her new date. She now understands the reason for her earlier, seemingly misplaced, bothersome premonitions. She feels she has warned herself through the dream to stay away from this new man. She feels relieved.

It should be noted that the suggestion to incubate a dream on a certain problem may not always work. Defining a problem to dream about may be difficult, particularly when one is not in a clear crisis situation, or when one is working alone without help. The problem one focuses on alone may not reflect one's real or deep concerns, and will therefore mislead. Moreover, even if the problem is correctly defined, incubation techniques may not succeed. They should be regarded merely as tools worth trying.

THE STRUCTURE AND LANGUAGE OF DREAMS

There is Method in this Madness.

Shakespeare

The Two Ways the Mind Works

Dreams are like an emotional scanner of the self, projected on the mind's screen. To "read" this screen one must know something about the construction of the enigmatic, symbolic, and metaphoric language of dreams. It is useful to regard the dream language as one part of the mind's dual processing system, the other part being the main mode of the awake state. These two information processing systems are based on different biochemical and electrical brain states, each equipped to deal with different sorts of information for different mental purposes. The language of the awake mind operates according to "secondary process thinking," so called because it is a way of thinking that develops later in childhood, after what is known as the infant's "primary process thinking." Secondary process thinking is the common public language of facts and figures, of categories and hierarchies, of cause and effect, of what is popularly called rational thinking. One of its most salient features is its capacity to abstract, to regard things for what they represent rather than for what they are. Secondary process sees a written word for its meaning, while disregarding the shape of the letters that construct that word.

In contrast, primary process thinking is the private language of direct experience. It is the language of children, poets, artists, of those who are mad, and of the dreaming brain. It handles sensory and perceptual information in a concrete rather than an abstract mode, seeing a thing for its primary qualities of shape, color, or texture, as well as for the emotional experience it evokes in the observer. Letters on a page, according to primary process, are mainly intricate drawings, and not just signs with meaning. The primary process is best equipped to capture the essence of the emotional experience, of "how things really feel."

Primary process thinking is nonsequential and nonlinear; it can jump with equal agility in any direction. It disregards the physical constraints of time and space, as well as the cause and effect rules of the sequential logic of secondary process thinking. Everything is possible in primary process, including the collection of data from seemingly unrelated domains like past and present, here and elsewhere.

This associative thinking, or the capacity to link seemingly unrelated domains, is the hallmark of both dreaming and creativity. Modern thinkers feel that the dreaming mind forms creative ideas precisely because it is operating associatively. It has been set loose to wander "mindlessly," creating "irrational" pictorial configurations and ingenious associations that otherwise would never come into being.

Art, literature, and even scientific discoveries have been spawned by dreams. One such famous discovery is that of Friedrich August Kekulé (1829–1896), a German chemist who was seeking the basic structure of the organic multi-carbon molecule. Until his era, scientists believed that organic chains could exist only in a linear form. One night, as Kekulé was dozing off ". . . the atoms were gamboling before my eyes . . . wriggling and turning like snakes. And see, what was that? One of the snakes seized its own tail and the image whirled scornfully before my eyes." Kekulé's dream-born sketches culminated in the discovery of the ring structure of the benzol carbon ring, thus revolutionizing the field of organic chemistry.

Alchemy into Chemistry **Kekulé's dream, which led to his discovery of the ring structure of the benzene carbon molecule, portrayed a snake swallowing its tail, an image that uncannily resembles the Ouroboros, a symbol of cosmic energy in alchemical manuscripts.**

 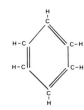

In sleep we are all painters, poets, and movie directors, because we are all creative, associative thinkers. Artists are endowed with the talent and determination to transform the unbridled imagery and elusive metaphor into actual structures of art. All people, however, are able to creatively tap the mystery and awe of their dreams, to translate the blend of primary and secondary raw symbols into a strong personal message. Here is an example.

> ### Drowning in Troubled Waters
> *Background:* An eighteen-year-old boy, on an extended trip away from home and facing age-appropriate questions about his future, had the following dream:
> *The dream:* I and somebody are talking about some guy named Bill Smith, some sort of an executive, who is writing a country-rock song titled "I Am Drowning in Troubled Waters." I know the words should be "Bridge Over Troubled Waters" but somehow the words have changed.
> *The dream work:* The dreamer had no clue as to what the dream meant. The dream decoding process produced the following relevant associations: *Bill Smith* was, for this dreamer, a synonym for "A nobody—my greatest fear in life is to be a nobody." An *executive* is "somebody who is supposed to have control over things." The association to *country-rock music* for the dreamer was "music of melancholy," and the mistake in the title of the song reminded him directly of his recent feelings of helplessness and turmoil about facing the future. Thus, the dream clearly portrayed his dread that his current moody state might be more powerful than his "executive" control and that he might "drown in his own troubled waters," that is, in his fear of being helplessly depressed and lost, and become a mere nobody.

The figure of "Bill Smith" has significance for the dreamer, both as a public American synonym for an "anybody" and hence a "nobody," and also as a personal feeling of what it is like to be a nobody—"my greatest fear in the world." The "executive" is a cultural symbol for control and management, but here it appears as a metaphor for management of the dreamer's personal internal affairs. Similarly, the distorted title of a well-known song and the dreamer's personal association to country music are combined to characterize the dreamer's prevailing mood, and to inform him of it in a manner much more vivid and compelling than a straightforward verbal statement such as "I feel depressed and potentially out of control and identity-less." When the young man had, with help, uncovered the dream's message, he was dumbfounded: "This is awesome. I couldn't think of a better way of describing these feelings myself." It was, of course, his self that did describe the feelings in his dream, using typical dream language.

It is important to realize that in almost all mental states and activities, both primary and secondary processes play their parts, simultaneously supporting each other. In fact, it is not easy to sort out and separate the pure form of either of the two processes. Only in extreme brain states, such as that of the drugged brain, the erratic mind of the madman, the as yet untutored, unprejudiced, half-finalized minds of infants, or the REM-dream state can we witness the operations of the primary process in its more distilled form.

Since dreams are expressed through primary processing, while the awake state, which attempts to decipher the dream's meaning, utilizes mainly secondary processing, a translation is required from one mode to another. In this sense, the work of dream interpretation can be defined as translating the material from the primary symbols of the dream language to the secondary symbols of awake language.

Fernand Khnopff's The Caress   **Khnopff's themes, like dreams, evoke timelessness, enigma, and perversity. The sphinx is a typical condensation used in dreams. As in many of his paintings, the proud chimera's head is that of his sister Marguerite, with whose beauty he was obsessed. Khnopff himself serves as the male model.**

How Dreams Construct Their Symbols

To understand how the dream constructs its symbols, one has to become familiar with what Freud called "the two architects of the dream": "condensation" and "displacement." These primary process mechanisms are not bound by the rules of logic, constancy of object, or unidirectional flow of time. In condensation, several ideas or images can be combined into one or, conversely, one object may be split into many fragments. One of the most common condensations is that of "hybrid people," that is, several people condensed into one. For instance, in "The Double Date" dream, the figure, who is simultaneously the dreamer's ex-husband and the new suitor, is a human hybrid that embodies an emotional message, clarifying for the dreamer her earlier premonitions, which had been difficult to understand in the awake state.

Condensation is so common in dreams that, in fact, it is unusual to find pure figures representing "just themselves." Certain compound figures, generally known as chimeras, such as the centaur (half horse, half human), the mermaid (half fish, half woman), the dragon (a winged serpent), or the sphinx (woman's face, lion's body, eagle's wings), and so on, are universal enough to have become cultural myths. They condense various expressive aspects and qualities into one, reminding us, as did Freud, that "the dream is a personal myth and myth is a dream of a culture."

The primary process has little respect for the common rules of language; words and sounds can be condensed irrespective of their logical meanings. Poets creatively, and babes and psychotics unintentionally, sometimes produce such "word chimeras" known as neologisms, newly "invented" words, like "mechtronic" (mechanical and electronic), or "famillionaire" (familiar and millionaire), based on rules and rhythms other than those of the logic of grammar. The following dream example illustrates how dreams utilize meaningful word condensations.

Airline to Lapland

Background: A patient who is struggling to become independent from his parents' influence recounts in therapy the following dream.

The dream: I am staying at my parents' place. I want to get away, to Lapland. I order a ticket through an airline, which, in the dream, my therapist owns. A plane lands in the back yard. It has a big name written on its side: ELP AIR-LINES.

The dream work: Lapland symbolized, for this dreamer, a kind of freedom and longed-for closeness to nature. The name of the airline is the dreamer's call and expectation for (H)ELP by the therapist, the owner of the plane, which can lift him out of his parents' influence and take him where he wants to go.

The second major mechanism of dreams is displacement: A psychic element, such as an object or an emotion, is lifted from its usual context and embedded in another. Displacement is the organizing principle of neurosis, jokes, aspects of creativity, and dreams, as well as metaphor. (In fact, the Greek word for "metaphor," *meta-pherine*, means "from one place to another.") Metaphor is the most expeditious and economical way of communicating an ambiance or an emotional point. By leaping between contexts, it bypasses the narrowness of common logic. Here is a dream example of displacement:

> **The Car Ride**
> *Background:* A woman with marital problems, of which she is only vaguely aware while awake, has the following dream.
> *The dream:* She is a passenger in the car her husband is driving. She worries that they will have an accident.
> *The dream work:* The car ride in this dream is quickly revealed to symbolize the dreamer's relationship with her husband, in which she harbors deep worries about his ability to steer a safe course.

The embodiment of something as complex and abstract as a relationship in a concrete image such as a car is a typical displacement maneuver of dreams. The metaphor captures a specific nuance or an entire range of emotional experience (in this case the woman's feeling unsafe with her husband) and succinctly reveals something that has been eluding the awake mind.

Unlike the common public symbols of secondary process, the dream's primary process symbols may have no meaning outside the personal realm and cannot be readily understood by others. Only the dreamer has the key to their meaning, as Heraclitus said two millennia ago: "The waking have one world in common; sleepers have each a private world of their own." This is why ready-made dream-symbol glossaries are largely meaningless. A horse in one man's dream can symbolize valor, while for another it can spell terror. Even one's own symbol can stand for different meanings in different dreams. The meaning of the symbol must emanate from the world of associations of the dreamer and not the prepared list of the interpreters, even if they are skilled masters. A snake is not necessarily a symbol of a penis, as Freud said, nor is it always a symbol of ancient wisdom, as Jung says myths imply. For a little girl who has been actually bitten by a snake and gone through a frightening hospitalization, a snake in a dream may represent that personal experience, and the more mythical, culturally general, meanings may not be relevant.

The Many Masks of the Self

Because of the erratic way the mind operates during REM sleep, and the garbled imagery of the dream, and because of the dreamer's waking wish to conceal what the dream attempts to reveal, it is not always easy to find one's self, or part of one's self, in the compound plot. When awake, the self is usually experienced as an indivisible whole, which ignores or minimizes certain undesirable or painful aspects. The dream's fantastic theater is the place in which the many varied sides of the self show. All figures, events, and even locations appearing in a dream may be aspects of the self, exhibited in a disguised form. And even though other people, sometimes completely unfamiliar, appear and perform in the dream, in the last analysis they all represent aspects of the dreamer. After all, you the dreamer are the playwright, the creator of the plot, as well as the director, player, and audience of this astonishing personal spectacle. A dream created by you is ultimately about you.

There are many ways to mask the self. The most common one is to split the dreamer into two or more roles, for instance, to make him or her both actor and spectator. One part is observing the other. The ''I'' may appear as someone else, as the ''other'' in the dream. In fact, it is safe to say that every ''other'' contains or hides some ''I,'' an aspect of the self, expressing itself. When an undesirable character in the dream doesn't seem remotely connected to one's self, it may seem easier to protest; ''That wasn't me. That was that stranger.'' But it was you after all, since you invented and cast the role of the other.

Ferdinand Hodler (1852–1918), *Night* **Night for Hodler was "the great symbol of death." In his first masterpiece, terror is well illustrated by the dreamer in the throes of a nightmare, being haunted by a dark, covered figure that oppresses the dreamer and seems to grow from within his own blanket.**

The Bank Robbery

Background: A young scientist, eager to make a name for himself in the scientific community, has the following dream while writing his Ph.D. dissertation.

The dream: Some accomplices and I are breaking into the safe vault of a bank, stealing a pile of shining jewels. I know we should take what we have and leave. If they find us, my reputation, my standing in society, everything I have worked for, will be lost. I tell my accomplices to leave, but they don't listen and want to grab more. We are caught in the act, and my heart sinks. I know everything is lost. There is a feeling of shame and despair.

The dream work: The bank vault and the jewels are the symbols for coveted recognition and fame. The entire *bank robbery scene* and the *greedy accomplices* represent the fear of the scientist of those greedy parts of his self that are fantasizing immoral shortcuts to scientific glory. On a deeper level, coveting "shiny valuables" just because they are considered highly by others, and the fear of being exposed and shamed for this falseness, creating the need to excessively defend against such wishes and fears, have been a lifelong aspect of this man's inner life, related, as usually is the case, to early childhood experiences.

Robert Vickrey (1926–), *Labyrinth* **Dreams, through their confounding labyrinthine paths, sometimes confront us with the hidden, dreaded part of ourselves, the part we usually try not to face, aptly named by Jung, the "shadow."**

Sometimes the place or location in which the dream occurs is the mask which hides the concealed aspect of the self.

Symphony Hall or Cheap Saloon
Background: A famous entertainer and TV personality has a dream, which
bothers him for several days.
The dream: The dreamer finds himself in a hall, half of which is a renowned
symphony hall, the other half a cheap entertainment saloon.
The dream work: In this dream, the two parts of the performance hall stand for
the two conflicted parts of the dreamer's professional self. One part of him
aspires to the esteemed status of the symphony hall, with its high-level art
and respectable recognition, but the requirements of which demand dedication
and serious effort. The cheap saloon represents his other part, the insecure
one, where he can get away with a cheap laugh but at the expense of the fear
of always remaining a two-bit, seedy entertainer, doing his cheap song-and-
dance routine. On a deeper analysis, these two disparate sides represent not
only his professional self but also the split structure of his entire self-esteem.

The Shadow Mask

Often only after decoding the dream does a person realize that he/she has met
the part of the self he/she would rather not know about. Jung aptly named that
covert part "the shadow," the dark side of the self. The shadow typically appears
as a monster or as a repulsive or unpleasant figure.

Though by definition an unlovable but unavoidable part of the self, the
shadow becomes terrifying only while it remains unrecognized. An unidentified
shadow can follow one through life and through dreams, undermining function
and terrifying sleep. When brought to light and confronted, it assumes everyday
proportions and, insofar as it is accepted, can actually be more easily controlled
than when hidden. For example, by confronting his greed and wish to take
shortcuts, the dreamer of "The Bank Robbery" dream has a good chance to
integrate and thereby control those shadowy aspects of himself.

Sometimes a person is not ready to meet his/her shadow. In that case,
even if the dreamer remembers and reports the dream, he/she will not be able
to understand its meaning. One has to be psychologically ready before the dream
code can be cracked.

Nightmares and Night Terrors

Dreams that cause fear and dread, among them frightening "shadow" dreams,
are known as bad dreams or nightmares. Although these REM-stage nightmares

can be terrifying, the term "night terrors" is reserved for non-REM stage III and IV events in which the sleeper has a frightening hallucination, wakes, or almost wakes, terrified, usually with a crushing sensation of the chest, and falls back to sleep retaining no waking memory of the event. While night terrors in adults are considered a sleep disorder, sometimes requiring pharmacological treatment, in children they are a normal developmental event, despite the drama, that passes after some time, and they need no special treatment.

Nightmares, in contrast to night terrors, are normal throughout life. Although some appear in non-REM sleep, those non-REM nightmares are experienced without clear plots and with vague imagery. REM-sleep nightmares are vivid, may have intricate plots, and like many other dreams of the REM phase often portray some unresolved psychological conflicts. There is no antidote for nightmares. Like all other dreams, they remind us of the depths and extremes of our emotions, and may carry a message or lesson through their frightful images.

Dreams Following Trauma

Dreams following trauma are biologically and structurally different from other dreams. Trauma occurs when an experience renders someone helpless—an experience induced either by other human beings or by nature—and cracks the envelope of safety and healthy denial, which is a necessary part of our mental armor. The result of trauma, the post-traumatic state disorder, produces, among other symptoms, recurring dreams that typically replay the traumatic event and cause the dreamer to awaken fighting or screaming. Dreams following trauma are special combinations of nightmares and night terrors, being extremely vivid dreams yet occurring in non-REM sleep. Post-traumatic nightmares can be repeated many times in a night, and are so exhausting that trauma victims, such as severely traumatized war veterans, may despair. With proper support and persistent therapy, these nightly tortures can gradually be alleviated.

Unlike the vivid dream replications of horrific events, which tend to follow adult trauma, dreams of adults traumatized in childhood are regular REM dreams, whose message of early trauma is difficult or impossible to recognize. The distance from childhood, the limited understanding of the child's mind at the time the painful event or repeated events occurred, as well as the adaptive demand to forget and go on with life, all have combined to screen those memories from awareness. Typical of childhood-trauma dreams in adults is the paucity of clues and the lack of an identifiable villain. Rather, there are fragments of suggestive symbols, which are hardly ever recognized without help. It is safer to have some expert guidance when one wishes to seriously explore such painful realms of childhood.

DECODING AND INTERPRETING

I know that if we meditate on a dream sufficiently long and thoroughly—if we take it about with us and turn it over and over—something almost always comes of it.

Carl Gustav Jung

The Raw Statement

For physiological reasons mentioned earlier, freshly remembered dreams will usually evaporate faster than morning dew, within minutes, unless preserved in some form other than the unreliable, evanescent screen of pictorial dream memory. Even the most detailed dream image tends to dissipate unless transformed into another kind of memory storage system, that of words, preferably the written kind. The first step, therefore, in preserving dream memory is transferring dreams to the written word, the raw statement. The raw statement is your initial, confused, sleep-webbed statement, which you have scribbled in the middle of the night, or immediately upon waking in the morning. Its role is to catch the dream before it evaporates. This initial statement is not committed to order, sense making, or calligraphic quality. As long as your handwriting is somewhat legible, you have performed your task. You have provided the rough draft, the raw stuff, your memory link to the story "the way it happened."

The raw statement should include as many dream details as possible. Put down everything. Try to be faithful to the dream's events and images. Don't hesitate to use examples or any associations that come to mind: "Her hair is long and smooth like that of my friend Jill" or "The house reminds me of my uncle's farm, where the entire family used to go every summer . . ."

When describing events and happenings it is important to use the present tense as much as possible, as if you are undergoing the same events at the moment: "I am *walking* in the street, and a man *comes* to me with something in his hand. At first it is hard to see, but as he *moves* his hand a bit closer, *I can* tell that he *is holding* a cane, somewhat like the bad guy in the movie last night. I *am turning* to run away but it is clear that he *is following* me . . ." The present-tense recounting is a simple and effective device for refreshing memory, used, for example, in hypnotic sessions aimed at memory reconstruction. It will increase the likelihood that you'll include as many details as possible.

The raw statement can be jotted directly into the Dream Diary section of *The Dreamland Companion,* with exceptions for space-saving. Dreamers of two dreams each night and/or those whose morning scribble tends to be expansive may choose not to consume the diary pages too fast and to have some blank paper at hand on which to scribble the raw statement first. Then, following one of the suggested decoding layouts, the dream can be rewritten in the Diary section.

Memory Enhancing
That memory, the warden of the brain, / Shall be a fume.

Shakespeare

Suggestive Techniques

The capacity for dream recall varies widely. Like the capacity for imagining or being hypnotized, it may reflect some biological tendency with regard to retention of vivid imagery. Poor dream recall may be the result of a long-standing habit of disregarding any information that is not couched in matter-of-fact external reality. But whether dream recall is easy or difficult, it is not a fixed capacity, and is somewhat subject to change. Certain life transitions, such as travel, moving, weddings, pregnancy, or painful loss and trauma, are likely to produce series of vivid dreams, reflecting the brain's attempt to integrate those changes.

There is a clear suggestive element to dream recall, which can be exploited. The mere proposal to dream by an authoritative figure, such as a therapist, may produce increased dream recall. Similarly, one can improve dream retention by heightening dream awareness—talking and reading about dreams, listening to the dreams of others, joining dream groups or circles, or going into therapy. Since the moment before falling asleep is a *hypnagogic* suggestive state, in which the mind is unhinged from its wakeful, logically driven thought routines, but has not yet sunk into the oblivion of deeper sleep, incubation, or the pre-sleep self-reminder to dream, can also be useful in promoting dream recall.

Technical Tips

Even with recall-persuading techniques, the physiology of memory dictates that a dream will evaporate rapidly. There is a universal tendency to "forget" this rule and give in to the temptation to postpone documentation. Several memory-anchoring tips are recommended.

1. *Avoid chemicals:* Alcohol, tranquilizers, and hypnotics (sleeping pills) are inhibitors of brain activity. Although they may facilitate falling asleep, they wreak havoc on the normal architecture of the REM/non-REM cycle, and interfere with normal dreaming physiology. Obviously, dream recall may be impaired following the ingestion of such chemicals.

2. *Keep the* Companion *and the pen within hand's reach:* If you are not at home, or if you prefer, you can keep a page or a notebook next to your bed wherever you are, so that you can write your raw statement, which can later be entered into the work pages of your *Companion.*

You may prefer to use a tape recorder or another sound-recording device such as a voice-activated dictaphone, which is on call all night and saves the trouble of excessive fiddling. Later on, the recorded dream can be transferred into writing as a raw statement or into one of the decoding layouts.

3. *Give yourself some recording time:* You need a few minutes for writing down the raw statement of your dream. Set your waking alarm so that you have a few extra minutes in which to reflect upon your dream, record it, talk about it, and enter it in the diary section. If you wake up and immediately turn toward the toothbrush instead of the pen, or storm out into a world of urgent obligations, you won't document your dream when you still can, and when you finally decide to capture some of its details, you'll have nothing to record.

4. *Buzz words:* If by any chance you are so pressed for time that you don't feel

you can afford to sit down and write the raw statement of an evocative dream you would like to remember, at least jot down, in the diary or anywhere, the main symbols, figures, or events that occurred in the dream, even as you rush off. For instance, if biblical Jacob, escaping from his wronged brother's wrath, had been in an immense hurry on waking from his dream, the words "ladder," "angels (up and down)," and "promised land," would have been found on his papyrus. The rest of the reconstructive work can be done later.

5. *Make your sleep partner your dream partner* if you are both amenable to the idea. Sharing dreams is an efficient as well as exciting way of remembering and even beginning the decoding process of the dream. Immediately after the telling of your dream, try and document it as a raw statement in the Diary section of the *Companion.* Sometimes both partners will have had dreams on the same night, which they want to share at the same time. The one who is doing the listening initially would be wise to jot down his/her dream's buzz words first; otherwise the dream may fade before it is his/her turn to talk.

Remembering dreams only infrequently need not be a source of disappointment. Daily entries in the diary are not demanded or expected. For most people, the normal interval between remembered dreams may be days, weeks, at times even months.

The Interrogation of the Dream

It has long been an axiom of mine that the little things are infinitely the most important.
Sherlock Holmes speaking for Arthur Conan Doyle

Now that the nocturnal raw statement is secure, you can begin the decoding process, immediately or some time later. Decoding is, in fact, an exciting game of minds you play with yourself. You split yourself into two distinct roles, that of the persistent interrogator and that of the amenable eyewitness. The interrogator is that part of you that wants to understand, but doesn't have the information. The interrogator's job therefore is to be persistent, relentlessly pursuing any crumb of data, as insignificant as it may seem, and trying, through the teasing of details and associations to these details, to make sense and order out of the puzzle. The eyewitness part of you holds the information key to the solution, even if you are not aware of it.

As the interrogator, you go over the report, sentence by sentence, item by item. You question everything. Any seemingly trivial occurrence may be important. It is useful also to think of the interrogator as an extraterrestrial, who is completely unfamiliar with your world and needs explanations for every detail. If your eyewitness says, "Oh, you know what I mean by a sports car," the extraterrestrial should not accept that answer but relentlessly repeat: "What, indeed, is a sports car? What is a sports car to you? What kind of sports car? Have you seen one before? What does it remind you of?" Asking one's self such seemingly simple questions is not easy when another part of you takes the answers for granted. As the eyewitness, you should answer in full detail, by saying, for example: "A sports car is small, fast, and dangerous, but also exhilarating. I have always wanted one . . .," an answer that may lead to the right emotional clue.

The details constitute the first category of information to look for. The dogged interrogator repeatedly asks for all details: Precisely *where* are you? Exactly *when* is it taking place? Specifically, *who* is with you and *who* does he resemble? Just *what* do they look like? With nuances, *how* do you feel and behave in the dream? (*WWWWH*). In order to encourage the production of details, the interrogator and the eyewitness try to keep to the present tense, as if visualizing events as they are happening. Although details may seem minute and insignificant, their importance cannot be overemphasized in triggering relevant associations. It is the color of the sports car or the shape of the pipe in the dream that may usher in the precise association necessary for the cracking of the dream's code or riddle. For example, if the color of the sports car is red, you wish to know what kind of red. The detailed response is essential, since it is that particular "glossy" or "dark" red that will lead to the appropriate association.

If you are inclined, drawing a dream can encourage the retention of the dream's details. You need not come up with an artistic document, but you'll have an important image, which can serve as a powerful reminder of the dream.

Associations, the most important data for the decoding process, are whatever comes to one's mind as a response to the events and images of the dream, no matter how unrelated or irrelevant they may seem. You the dreamer are the only one who has this data stored in the memory vaults of your entire lifetime. You are the only one who can provide these associations, the clues to your dream's meaning.

The particular shade of red that came up in the eyewitness's detailed statement can now be teased for associations. What is that "red" to you? What does it remind you of? You may discover surprising associations to that color from your deep personal memory. And although, for many people red stands for blood, passion, danger, or aggression, for a particular dreamer red could mean comfort, because the draperies in his/her nursery were red. In essence, it is always necessary to know what the particular detail means to the particular dreamer. Very often, there will be more than one association to a dream's detail, which need not worry you. An assortment of associations provides a rich display from which to choose an interpretation, and often even disparate associations are consistent with the same interpretation.

The supremacy of the dreamer's own associations over dream-symbol glossaries cannot be overstated. Readymade clues for the solution of dream riddles at best provide generalized probabilities within a given culture. They can serve as useful or interesting bases for comparison between the dreamer's individual world and the cultural world in which he or she lives, but they cannot replace the individual association and its meaning in that particular dream.

Associations can be categorized according to current associations or depth associations. Current associations are those dream details associated with "day residues," those actual events, objects, or figures that were encountered during the day or days preceding the dreams. Thus, if you saw your old teacher on the street or noticed a green house near a parking lot, these may find their way into your dream the following night or nights. They are some of the everyday pieces the dream uses to create its puzzle.

Current associations may be aroused as a response to day-residue detail in the dream, or to any other detail. Current associations connect your dream to the prevailing moods and issues of recent life events.

Depth associations are related to one's core issues, transcending immediate life events. They usually connect present events or states of mind to former moods and emotions, spanning from childhood to the present. Depth associations dig deeper into the structure of one's being and provide more general statements about one's hidden aspects.

Let us examine the following dream from the point of view of current and depth associations.

The Speechless Speaker

The dream's raw statement: I am the third speaker in a big conference. After the intermission, it is my turn to speak. I get up, face the huge audience, an ocean of faces, and suddenly I realize that I don't know what to say. I glance at my notes. They are blank. The crowd is getting impatient. It is obvious that I have to say something, anything, and yet it is equally clear to me that there is nothing I can say. *I don't know what to say.* I feel an awful sense of having neglected my duty, and do not know how to get out of this terrible situation. At this point, I wake up, feeling, to my surprise, resolve and relief, because I immediately know what the dream refers to.

Current associations: The dreamer is initially aware that the day-residue trigger for the dream is a rather routine lecture he is to deliver in front of his students the next morning. His next association, also of the current type, is to a more important lecture, on the same topic, that he is supposed to deliver to the distinguished audience of his professional association, in a few weeks time. His place in the order of speakers within the dream, third, after the intermission, matches exactly what his place in the order of speakers will be at the professional conference. This he knows because he received a notice about that conference just recently. The upcoming professional lecture is an important one, for which he has been delaying or denying the need for preparation, calming himself by rationalizing that he is familiar with the subject matter from his routine lectures to his students.

The relief felt on waking is also a crucial clue. He recognizes what he wouldn't acknowledge all along, that he has fears of not being ready and being shamed in front of his colleagues, and that, in contrast to the dream situation, he is still in a position to salvage things, i.e., to prepare thoroughly for the important lecture.

Depth associations: When asked to associate to the sense of speechlessness and helplessness in front of a looming, expectant audience, the dreamer was reminded of a similar, familiar feeling lacing his entire life since early childhood: the feeling of always being center stage, in the limelight, of having to perform to the expectations of others. The seduction to perform as a means of gaining approval and admiration was an ever-present part of his being, always accompanied by that barely noticeable sense of dread that he might fail the expectations, disappoint the audience, and find himself in an intolerably shameful situation. Suddenly, it is not only the professional lecture that is the issue at hand, but also a lifelong emotional position and personal style that are illuminated by the dream. A core motif that has been motivating and dictating this man's life has been exposed.

Depth associations are not always readily elicited; when they are revealed, however, they convey valuable, penetrating insights. Once a correct depth association has been reached, a self-truth has been touched and is then available for repeated examination, which can help one either modify a particular trait or accept it more gracefully.

The Decoding Layouts

Special page layouts may enhance the decoding process providing an easier way to add details and associations. Three different layouts, using the "Drowning in Troubled Waters" dream, are suggested below. They illustrate different organizational options to boost the memory and associative process. With time, you can combine elements of each or come up with a system of your own that works best for you.

<u>Layout 1: Center Page</u>

The raw statement is written in the center of the page, while the additional details of the interrogation and associations are jotted down along the wide margins on all four sides.

hidden, dangerous?

someone *who is in charge. I am not in charge.*

I and somebody, he is in (the dark,) I can't see him, are talking about some guy named (Bill Smith,) who is in some sort of an (executive,) who is writing a country (rock song) titled "I Am (Drowning in Troubled Waters)." I know the words should be "bridge over troubled waters", but somehow the words have changed.

anybody, nobody! I have always had a great fear of being a nobody

sad, melancholy song.

the way I feel right now! My emotions are flooding me.

Layout 2: Color Coding

Rewrite separately each of the raw statement sentences, followed by the details and associations to that sentence that arise through the interrogator/eyewitness technique. Differentiate between current and depth association by highlighting each type in a different color marker.

In this example, blue represents current associations and pink represents depth associations. Now let's rewrite the dream's statement with added details and the associations:

"I and somebody are talking about some guy named Bill Smith."

I don't know exactly where we are, or who the guy next to me is. I can't see his face. As for Bill Smith, he looks ordinary. Bill Smith reminds me of a nobody, all the nobodies of this world. The thing I fear most is to be a nobody. I have been fighting all my life not to show how ordinary I sometimes feel. I guess I have been feeling like that recently.

"Bill Smith is some sort of an executive, who is writing a country rock song titled 'I Am Drowning in Troubled Waters.' "

An executive is somebody who is supposed to be in control of things. I would like to be in executive control of my life, but I don't feel I am in control of much lately. Country music always makes me feel sad, and this particular song, a sadder version of the Paul Simon song, with the words changed, from "bridge over" to "drowning in," makes me feel so sad and helpless I feel like crying. I guess this is not a new feeling. I think I have been living with it for many years, but now it is all coming out because I am away from home.

Layout 3: Split Page

In this design, the dream statement is written on the left half of the page, while the relevant additional details and associations are then recorded on the right side. The first section of the "Drowning in Troubled Waters" dream is shown as an example for this layout system.

I and somebody are talking about a guy named Bill Smith.	Bill Smith is an anybody or a nobody. The thing I fear most is to be a nobody.

When No Associations Come to Mind

Having no associations to the events or images in the dream is a common difficulty. The dreamer feels stuck and exasperated, after having racked his/her brain in vain. There is a tendency at this stage to give in to the fallacy that "no association" means that the dream's symbol is meaningless, and to abort the dream work altogether. It might help the dreamer at this point to remember that there is a universal conflict between wanting and not wanting to know what the dream attempts to uncover. If the dream's image is vivid or haunting, but the well of associations to it is dry, this may be a sign that the side that doesn't want to know has the upper hand and is subduing a meaningful message.

At this point the dreamer can make the decision to try once more, reviewing the raw statement slowly and thoroughly. What is needed is a deliberate rerun of the dream work, looking for more details, which may yield hidden associations. Persistence will often circumvent the wish-not-to-know side.

Here is an example of being stuck and getting unstuck by trying once more.

The Woman with the Missing Eyebrows

Background: A woman in her forties had a dream that bothered her. Not being able to produce even one meager association, she asked some dinner companions, who were experienced in the art of dream interpretation, for help.

The dream: "I dreamed I was looking at my reflection in the mirror and saw that I had no eyebrows. I woke up feeling troubled, although, for the life of me, I can't see what the dream means, or what relevance it has for me, and yet a strange and heavy feeling lingers on."

The dream work: She was asked to go over the decoding process step by step. When she described again the missing eyebrows, she was asked for more details. At first she responded. "What details? There were no eyebrows, period!" In response to an undaunted persistent demand to describe what the missing eyebrows looked like, she said, "Well, there were actually some traces of eyebrows, remnants of sparse blond hair, and a dark thin pencil line on top." Did that new detail remind her of anyone? "Of course! I recently had a house guest for five weeks who walked around just like that, with that silly pencil line instead of eyebrows. All my friends kept talking about how ridiculous she looked." What is the quality she associates with that person most? "Well, I guess it was that mask look, a kind of falseness that I found hard to bear." From here on, the interpretation came gushing: "I guess the dream is telling me that I share some of that woman's qualities, a kind of falseness that I know I have too." Her eyes became moist and reflective. After a few minutes, she smiled through her tears and said, "Well, maybe it's unpleasant, but at least it is the truth. It is easier to know what you are facing than not being able to name it."

The deliberate review of the details of the dream pushed the woman past her block, enabling her to associate the missing eyebrows with the house guest, and to link both to her own sense of falseness. Incidentally, at that tearful moment of self-awareness she was completely free of any traces of falseness.

If the deliberate rerun is performed conscientiously and there is still no trail to follow, one can try the method of interviewing the dream characters. This could even be done in writing, like a formal documented dialogue. It could open an unexpected trail of associations unavailable through the regular probing technique. For instance, the woman in the eyebrow dream could have had the following written exchange with her eyebrowless dream reflection:

Woman: Who are you?

Reflection: Don't you know?

W: Why do you have no eyebrows? Why do you tweeze your eyebrows?

R: Is it a problem for you?

W: Yes! It infuriates me.

R: Why?

W: Because it looks just like that ridiculous guest of ours, silly and false.

From here on the interpretation flows as before.

It is not unlikely that the same theme you are struggling with in a current dream has been trying to show itself in different guises. Therefore, when unable to find any associative direction, looking for similar structures or motifs in recent dreams may be helpful. There are two kinds of serial dreams phenomena: repeated dreams and dream series.

The repeated dream is simply evidence that one's basic issues continue to seethe, seeking to be recognized and resolved. Repeated dreams may wear different costumes, but they reenact the same basic play, which is usually a core issue for the dreamer, or some problem that is currently on her/his mind. Typical repeated dreams include themes such as failing or not being prepared at an important moment, shadow dreams where the undesirable "shadow" aspect of the self reappears, instances of being exposed and shamed, etc. Repeated dreams can appear in the same night, the same week, the same period, or may occasionally resurface throughout a lifetime.

In a dream series, two or more different dreams appearing around the same time may share a common theme, reflecting the mind's attempt to throw varying light beams on the same unresolved issue. Each dream in a dream series may shed light on the others, and each also marks the developmental steps toward achieving resolution of the problem at hand, as in the following series:

Dream I *The Burgled Room*
Background: A happily married woman is having multiple complications and bleeding during her second pregnancy. She is hospitalized and it is not sure the pregnancy will last.
The dream: I am in the house, but something is very wrong in one of its rooms. The windows have been broken, and there is a terrible mess inside that room. It could have already been burgled. I don't know what to do. I feel frightened.
The dream work: The *troubled room* is her womb, and the fear is directed at the impending loss of what is inside, which is already in a precarious state.

Dream II *The Glass Shards*
Background II: Two days later, as her bleeding continued, she was faced with a conflict—whether to continue the pregnancy, at a risk to her life, or to abort. She then had a new dream.
Dream II: I hear my three-year-old child cry at night, and I want to get out of bed to go to him, but I am barefoot, and the entire floor is covered with shards of glass. I don't know what to do. I feel frightened and helpless.
The dream work: Here, the needs of the living child and the health of the mother are threatened by the dangerous situation, the glass shards, which may cause her to bleed to death. The dream does not resolve the conflict, but reflects, with its compelling imagery, the terrible emotional dilemma this woman is facing.

Dream III *The Baby Is Dead*
Background III: A few days later, the bleeding complications seem to have stopped, but the pregnant woman has another dream. A day after this dream she has a miscarriage.
Dream III: The nurses come and tell me the newborn baby is dead. I am not surprised since I have been expecting this news. I just go into the room where

the baby is lying, kiss his brow, and say goodbye to him, without fear and without crying.

The dream work: The dream conveys to the woman that the baby is lost, even before the actual miscarriage occurs. It is not uncommon for dreams to pick up distress signs of the body before they are physically manifested. The dream also informs the woman that she has already mourned this inevitable loss, and that she can go back to life without fear. This time, when the message is clear and accepted, there is very little need for metaphors and the dream's language is simple and realistic.

This dream series is a consecutive report from the inner emotional world of a woman struggling with a life-endangering situation that produces deep fears and conflicts. Each dream reflects these apprehensions and conflicts and at the same time helps the understanding of these issues. Each dream enhances the message of the other dreams as well. In two of these dreams the woman uses the common symbol of the house with rooms as an illustration of the self and its various aspects.

Dream partners or dream teams are always useful aids in the illumination of a dream's message. This is not to say that one cannot grasp alone the essence of certain dreams, but any dream analysis can benefit from a second opinion, or rather a second questioning. Whether naive or sophisticated, the question posed by someone other than you may lead the decoding process in the right direction. The partner relieves you of the interrogator's role, allowing you to concentrate on being the eyewitness. Another person may puzzle at certain details, or insist on further clarification of issues your avoidant side might be unconsciously trying to ignore.

No matter how expert you become, or how many experts or techniques you employ, there's always a dream that will remain only partially solved, or not solved at all. At times, despite all troubleshooting efforts, you may feel completely stuck. You needn't be discouraged. The dream can be stored and solved later. When a dream's code remains uncracked, just leave it as it is in the Dream Diary section and mark it as an unsolved dream in the Calendar-Index section. At another time, when you have honed your skills or have become readier for the dream's message, you can review your diary and try again. Even if you never solve a dream, however, if the topic is important it will resurface in another guise, giving you other chances to explore that part of you trying to be heard.

Choosing the Correct Interpretation

Since every detail or part of a dream may give rise to more than one association, sometimes there are different options for interpretation. Which interpretation should you choose? How do you know an interpretation is true?

At times there is more than one correct dream interpretation. For instance, the speechless speaker dream is correctly interpreted both as a warning to prepare for the important lecture and as a reminder that an old emotional pattern has not been resolved. At other times, there is only one right interpretation, which can be distinguished from the misleading ones by using the emotions as a guide. There is an Aha ! sensation informing you that you are unmistakably there. Feelings never mislead, once they are clear. The best interpretation is the conclusion or realization, arrived at from the association, that feels most relevant.

The Aha! feeling, leading to the correct interpretation, may arise from the day residue, from a current association to it, from a depth association, or from all of these realities, which are intricately intertwined. Common dream actions as flying, falling, forgetting, or facing diverse circumstances are good examples for the possible realities out of which the dream is created and experienced. Falling, for instance, can be a mere byproduct of the activation of motor-command centers in the dreaming brain. When only this is so, the dream will probably evoke no associated emotion. Falling or flying can also be related to a day residue, such as stumbling, which, for some reason, was captured by the subliminal memory. Dreams of falling could also contain a warning about some potential literal fall, as in the falling-off-a-ladder dream of a woman who that day had begun painting her kitchen. After waking, she examined the ladder and discovered that one of its rungs was loose, a detail she had apparently registered subconsciously the day before and then brought to her attention in her dream.

Flying or falling can also stand as symbols for a prevailing mood or situation, as in the dream of a worker, in which he fell down the stairs of his office building, reflecting his current fears that his work was deteriorating, in other words, that he was "falling down on the job." Finally, falling can illustrate a deep, ongoing sense of failure, which fits the archetypal meaning. In this case, there is congruence between the personal and the universal. Where the personal and the universal interpretations differ, the personal always prevails, as illustrated by the dream of a young woman whose "car fell into a lake." When teased for details, which always provide the relevant clues, she described the falling as "gentle" and the lake as "calm and beautiful." For this woman, the dream reflected her deep feeling that the inner journey she was making was right for her; that if she would let herself fall, instead of fighting the experience, she would land safely on the waters of her unconscious world. Similarly, flying, which is generally considered a symbol of positive feelings such as relief, elation, freedom, or rising above an obstacle, can at times express negative emotional states, such as going too high too fast, or being aloof, experiencing disconnected loneliness, as in the dream of a newly divorced airline pilot, in which he was hovering way above all the little people below. His flying was a defensive maneuver against feeling small, abandoned, and hurt.

Difficult Themes to Interpret: Death, Illness, and Sex

Death and Illness Dreams

Emotions are usually reliable guides through the maze of dream interpretations. With certain sensitive subjects, however, such as illness, death, and sex, which reflexively arouse fear, guilt, or shame, these emotions may actually mislead. Dreams that include death, either the death of the dreamer or someone close to him or her, are particularly powerful anxiety provokers. The vividness of the dream's reality can arouse a sense of premonition: "Am I dreaming my own death?" or "Am I wishing my mother's death?" Some will swear that their death-theme dreams foretold an actual death that later occurred in real life.

Death dreams can either manifest anticipation of actual mourning and sorrow, or symbolically reflect change and loss, but, as far as we know, in every case they tell us "what we feel" rather than "what will happen." Dreams of death or dead ones often project fears of one's own mortality, and are common when someone close to the dreamer has died, or on an anniversary of a death. The "Joining the French Foreign Legion" dream of the elderly professor is an example of mortality issues raised after the death of a friend. At times of life-threatening illnesses, dreams capturing the hope for life and the fear of death are particularly abundant and often include images of the dreamer struggling through scenes of catastrophes, like wars, earthquakes, fires, and so on. Such dreams are sometimes accompanied by a strong conviction that the dreamer is summoned to the world of the dead. When some time later the dreamer is still very much alive and perfectly healthy, he or she may recognize that the dream portrayed the fear of death rather than any actual fate.

At times of impending loss and grief, dreams usually reflect the struggle between acceptance and denial of the inevitable loss.

> ### Going to Los Angeles
> *Background:* A husband, who has been nursing his wife for many years during her slow but relentless malignant illness, had a dream several weeks prior to her death.
> *The dream:* A limousine is stopping in front of the house. The wife turns to him and says she has to leave for Los Angeles. She kisses him goodbye and steps into the vehicle. He is left standing as the car departs.
> *The dream work:* The dreamer was moved and puzzled by this short dream. "There is no one we know in Los Angeles," he said. "I couldn't think why she would want to go there." When asked to translate Los Angeles into English ("The Angels"), he became pale and tearful. This was his first explicit admission that death was winning the long battle and that separation was unavoidable and imminent.

Separation is difficult to accept, and while during daylight business one behaves in accordance with the reality of loss, during the dream state the feeling mind is not bound to the reality principle, and the longing for the deceased invokes his/her figure on the mind's REM-ing screen. The image of the dead person is not bound by time or space, and that figure may appear as he/she was at any age or stage in life. The image of the deceased may appear in dreams for weeks, months, and even years after death.

Many times death dreams have nothing to do with actual death or even physical danger. As in tarot cards, death is often a symbol for a turning point or a change that has occurred in the old self or is needed. For instance, it may reflect the fear or grief that the lively, carefree part of the self has not been

developed or is not accomplishing its healthy or intended function. It can also reflect a wish to be rid of an aspect of one's self, like the passive part, as in the dream of a man who was desperately trying to discard a dead doll that he was dragging behind him.

People dream not only that they are dying, but also that they are throwing their parents off the train, or their children off the roof, or strangling partners and shooting friends. That these dreams have not much to do with actual murderous intents is easily proved by the fact that often the dreamer's parents may already be dead or their children not yet born. Even when these dreams are generated by a recent or a long-standing nucleus of real anger, resentment, or guilt directed at the other person, they are not predictions of behavior but rather indications that such feelings exist.

Furthermore, it is useful to remember that all the actors in the dream are part of the dreamer's self. Thus, destroying a family member or friend may be a wish to be rid of some trait shared with that person. Likewise, parenticide in dreams may deal with the internalized aspect of the parent one wishes to destroy, while killing a child or a baby, or witnessing the death of a child usually has more to do with anger, guilt, or mourning over the child within one's self than it does with actual offspring, even if the dreamer is a parent.

Illness in dreams, like death, can be indicative of subliminal fears or suspicions of actual illness and/or symbolic of invalidism in a part of the self. At times, dreams can reflect actual physical problems even before the disease is diagnosed. The free-floating intuition of the dream will pick up the subtlest of physical signs and signals, which the awake mind tends to ignore or deny.

> **Sweet Blood**
> *Background:* A middle-aged physician had a dream prior to his yearly physical checkup.
> *The dream:* One of my patients, who has a blood disease, is on a tree, licking honey from the beehive, while the bees are swarming menacingly all over him.
> *The reality:* The next day, the physician was found to have diabetes, with high levels of blood sugar.
> *The dream work:* As a physician, this man had felt for a while that something was out of order with his bodily functions, yet he ignored all those suspicious signs. The dream condensed the image of the blood-diseased patient with that of honey, providing the diagnosis of a high level of sugar in the blood, or

diabetes. This doctor-dreamer must have made this diagnosis in his unconscious mind even prior to the blood test. The beehive scene on the tree, very much like the one of Winnie-the-Pooh, also evoked associations to his childish denial and irresponsibility, and to the consequences that awaited him.

It pays to heed one's illness dreams. Whether on the psychological or the physiological level, the dream may be signaling that something is not wholesome in one's system.

During pregnancy, although it is not an illness, disturbing dreams are common. While they may reflect physical problems of the pregnancy, as in "The Burgled Room" example, they may also symbolically represent the great adjustments in both body and soul demanded by this state. Dreams of the first trimester may be typically about an illness or a tumor growing inside, or about giving birth to an animal, an egg, or a monster instead of a human baby. The baby may appear deformed or painted blue. These dreams, which the father may share as well, reflect worries about not being ready for such a change of role in life, or the fear that something might go wrong during the pregnancy, and they are portraying the mind's attempt to integrate the upheaval. In the third trimester, dreams may focus on scenes of catastrophes, accidents with physical damage, and bodily dangers in general, reflecting fears of the birth itself as a potentially dangerous passage for both the mother and the child.

Bidden and Forbidden Sex Dreams

Much has been written about the symbolic level of repressed sexuality in dreams, to the point where, after Freud, every pencil was regarded with phallic suspicion until proven otherwise. Like dreams of death or illness, sex dreams reflect both physical and psychological preoccupations. They may arise during periods of sexual deprivation, just as food dreams may arise at times of hunger, or illness dreams when the body isn't well. The blatant sexual passions and candid sexual practices that often appear in dreams are first and foremost reminders that dreams, like sexuality, are rooted in physiology. During REM sleep, there is frequently an erection in males and clitoral engorgement in females. Wet dreams, those nighttime emissions common in males, are part of the psychophysiological equilibrium that keeps working even as we sleep. Like any other bodily feelings of ease or disease, which are woven into the web of the nightly plots during sleep, so sexual feelings make their way into dreams, to the delight or dismay of the dreamer. If such sexual dreams are pleasurable and not disturbing, one need only enjoy them.

Whether the sexual plot is ecstatic, pleasurable, unpleasant, or downright abhorrent, the rule of thumb about the dream's meaning, regardless of its sexual nature, remains the same as with other dreams that portray likely or unlikely activities. If the dream's emotional after effect is puzzling, disturbing, or haunting, then the dream is attempting to convey some issue, sexual or otherwise, that has not yet been resolved and integrated.

As an illustration, let us examine a dream of Julius Caesar two thousand years ago, recorded by Suetonius: "When . . . much to his dismay, Caesar had a dream of raping his own mother, the soothsayers greatly encouraged him by their interpretation of it: namely, that he was destined to conquer the earth, our Universal Mother."

The soothsayers of Caesar's time were already aware that dreams operate by symbolic displacement, and that a mother in a dream can symbolize the earth, and that rape can stand for any conquest by force. That, added to their knowledge of the ambitious character of Julius Caesar, gave them the ability to conjure an interpretation that was plausible as well as pleasing to him, since it allayed the shame and horror of the dream's literal plot, replacing them with grandeur and glory. However, had they paid attention to Caesar's distress with the goal of understanding it rather than simply allaying it, they might have interpreted the dream as reflecting Caesar's conflict, much documented elsewhere, about a forced and forbidden conquest of his own Roman republic, his motherland.

Like Caesar, we may all find ourselves, in our dreams, in "compromising" scenes, where we are cohabiting with friends, relatives, strangers, or nonhuman creatures, of the same or opposite sex, or witnessing sexual scenes that are highly irregular to our conscience, self-image, or background. Such troubling dreams indicate a struggle, but they are as likely to be unrelated to sex as they are to be about sexual activity. Since it is sexual passion that enables reproduction and creation, the appearance of the sexual theme in dreams often portrays the energy and passion of creativity and productivity. The sexual partner in the dream, like any other dream figure, may stand for a part of the self that is invigorated or wishing to be invigorated with passionate life forces.

Oral Sex in the Study

Background: A heterosexual married man, somewhat alarmed, found it difficult to relate the following dream.

The dream: I half open the door to my study and I see my brother and my best male friend performing oral sex. They look like one unit, like a living statue. It was my friend who was active, while my brother was the recipient of the act. They are so engrossed in their act that they don't notice me. I close the door softly and, somewhat to my amazement, instead of being shocked (after all, they are both "straight" and they hardly know each other), I find myself saying, "If that's what's important to them, let them do it without interruption."

The dream work: His main associations: *The study:* The place where I think, write, where I use my head. It is also the place of many frustrations lately, as I find myself passive and unable to perform my tasks the way I should be doing.

The brother: He is a passionate, suffering man, passive in some ways. He always feels he is not doing what he should be doing. He keeps saying he will act, but he is stuck in many ways. I definitely share some of these traits. *The friend:* He is very balanced, and wise. He knows his priorities. On the other hand, he is not so passionate. *Oral sex:* Basically, a very pleasurable practice in my marriage, and one that is mutually satisfying for me and my wife.

Based on these associations, the interpretation followed that in the patient's head (his study), two aspects of his personality are attempting to reach harmony and mutual satisfaction. The passionate but suffering and somewhat passive and guilty part is pleasurably joined by the more balanced, active part. This joining should be allowed to proceed uninterrupted until satisfaction—that is, until equilibrium is reached.

Indexing

When you have completed decoding and interpreting a dream, create a succinct summary and give the dream a title in order to crystallize the main elements and conclusion of the dream for future reference. The summary may be brief, but should contain the essential message. The title is an integral part of the dream work, and to function best as a reminder, it should be not only informative but also catchy if possible. The titles of the dream examples in this book may serve as illustrations. The summary and title should be written above the raw statement. In this way, one can browse through the diary's pages and be quickly reacquainted with a dream's content, or with several dreams of a given period. Below is an example of a summary and a title.

Title: **Drowning in Troubled Waters.**

Summary: My current fears are that my executive active powers will drown in my own depression, and my worst fear, that of being a Bill Smith, a nobody, will be realized.

At the head of the layout, add the date, and even the place where the dream was dreamt, if that is not your usual sleeping/dreaming place. Thus, the troubled waters dream would go in its owner's diary as:

2/3/91 **Drowning in Troubled Waters** *Spoleto, Italy—on the road.*

Now, move to the Calendar-Index section at the end of this book. Copy the dream title and page number in the appropriately dated square. In the Calendar-Index section the title can be shortened for space-saving purposes. Now you can retrieve that dream at any time with ease.

The year and month are not preprinted on the Calendar-Index pages, so you can begin using the diary at any time during the year. If you wish, you can note in the date squares any special or important dates, such as holidays, birthdays, anniversaries, trips, separations, and so forth. The Calendar-Index system is a form of synopsis for dreams' contents and life events, all put into one visual field. It enables the easy retrieval of any specific dream, and it provides a bird's-eye view of dreams during any given period. Now you can look for and identify possible patterns of dreaming, either by a common thread in the dream plots or by a correlation to the dates and life events of that period.

Feel free to improvise on the Calendar-Index system according to your needs or inclinations. For example, you may choose to code your dreams according to themes, such as nightmares, pleasant, erotic. Or you may use the criteria meaningful vs. trivial. You may code those dreams that have, to your opinion, been fully decoded, partially decoded, or those that have remained unsolved. You may code by symbol or by color. The degree of detail and amount of cross-referencing are entirely up to you.

Conclusion: A Never-ending Story

The *Companion*'s Diary is not a production report, for which you must fill a quota. It is a logbook of an extended journey, a companion to reflect the mind's longitudinal processes stretching over months and years. Sometimes, in the course of that journey, you may discover certain issues that you wish to understand more fully, and, at such a time it may be worthwhile to enhance the exploration by turning to psychotherapy. If the dream is a self-mirror, the therapist can be the mirror's mirror, adding an invaluable dimension to self-understanding. In this sense, while the *Companion* is an excellent introduction to the self, it is not a substitute for other, deeper ways of searching for the self. Moreover, therapy can facilitate the understanding of dreams themselves. You may be the author, producer, and director of your dream, but sometimes you alone cannot make the most profound sense of what that dream means. While it is true that without you no therapist can make a serious interpretation of your dream, it is also true that without a therapist you may not make as deep a one.

As with any journey, the experience is richest when the mind remains open to what the road unfolds. To maintain such an open spirit, however, is not easy, given the natural wish to try to predetermine the course, and the availability of techniques promising to fulfill the wish to control. Lucid dreaming is an example of such a seductive technique. Lucid dreaming means, very simply, being aware of dreaming during the dream itself. This is not an uncommon phenomenon recognized by many cultures, and, from a physical point of view, it probably reflects the shallowness of sleep during the dream state. The mixture of the boundless imagination of the dream state together with the observation power of the semi-aware self has attracted the imagination of mystics and researchers alike, leading to claims in recent years that lucid dreaming can be used for seizing control of the dream's content and changing its course and ending. For instance, one can learn to turn in one's dream to face a pursuer rather than flee. Such manipulation of the dream has been presented as a way of combating nightmares, but claims have also been made that such dream control can lead to better waking control over one's weaknesses, creative blocks, or other undesirable traits.

While it is true that one's fears and weaknesses are portrayed in dreams, the claims that altering the dream's content will change those fears and frailties are, at best, simplistic, and at worst, dangerously distorting. Such a claim can be likened to the assertion that if you retouch the photograph in your album, you will become a better-looking person. To add insult to injury, the lucid-dreaming training required to achieve dream control is an arduous, night-spoiling, and fun-spoiling exercise that in the end promises no real control over something that is not meant to be controlled in the first place. Alterations in plot endings are a natural occurrence, experienced by most dreamers at certain times, particularly if the dreamer continues a dream after having awakened in its midst and fallen asleep again. Then he/she may continue or repeat a pleasurable dream, or try to end an unpleasant dream in a different manner, like turning to fight back instead of fleeing a pursuer. To turn such a natural event into a forced practice, however, is inefficient and misses the mark.

Rather than "seizing control" by changing dreams, which is an elaborate way of avoiding internal messages, one should let go, open up, and listen. True "control" in order to make improvements or overcome blocks is best achieved in the aware awake state, having understood what one's dream is attempting to convey. Since dreams mirror rather than determine reality, if and when an internal change occurs, one's dreams will reflect that change. The many levels of the dream correspond to the levels of the self. Having arrived at one interpretation you may be at the beginning and not at the end of the road.

May you have interesting dreams.

Let diaries, therefore, be brought in use.

Francis Bacon

René Magritte (1898–1967),
La Reproduction Interdite ("Not to be Reproduced") (Portrait of Edward James) **A dream is a mirror of the hidden self. Because this mirror reveals precisely those emotional themes that the consciousness of the dreamer may be trying to conceal, self-interpretation of dreams can be difficult and has been compared to trying to see one's own back.**

I never travel without my diary. One should always have something sensational to read in the train.

Oscar Wilde

Simone dei Crocifissi (14th century), *The Dream of the Blessed Virgin* **Mary's dream of Jesus crucified on a tree growing from within her foretells the life of Christ.**

Erwin Shenkelbach (1930–   )
The Secret   **The half-hidden, half-inquisitive self, is captured here by a photographer who uses many of the mechanisms that operate in dreams to create his pictures.**

Ilan Kutz (1944–   ), *Black Knight's Move*   **On the chessboard of the mind, the shadow and light parts of the self (the dark and white horse both grow from the same stem) are engaged in a life-and-death combat. It is the turn of the shadow to attack, to the horror of the recoiling white knight.**

Rembrandt Harmensz van Rijn (1606–1669), *Jacob Wrestling with an Angel* **The Old Testament's report of Jacob's nightlong struggle with a "stranger" can best be understood as a dream about his struggle with his inner self.**

Jacob Confronting His Fear
Deliver me, I pray thee, from the
hand of my brother, from the hand of
Esau.(Genesis 32:11)

Gustav Doré (1832–1883), trilogy
**The relationship between crises
and dreams is illustrated in the
sequence of these three biblical
pictures. In the first scene, Jacob
is praying on the banks of the
river before meeting his feared
brother. The second picture,
though not formally recognized
as a dream, shows Jacob's
nocturnal struggle with a
messenger-angel, who at dawn,
like a dream, departs, leaving
Jacob with a new symbolic
name. Now he is confident about
the meeting with his dreaded
brother, which, as the third
picture shows, goes well. This
series illustrates the importance
of confronting the messenger of
the inner self.**

And Jacob was left alone; and there
wrestled a man with him until the
breaking of the day. (Genesis 32:24)

And Esau ran to meet him, and
embraced him . . . (Genesis 33:4)

Kinuko Craft (1940–),
The Reflection **Who created the
other—the woman with the
brushes in her hair, floating
above, or the woman with the
brush in her hand, floating
below? Aristotle likened dream
imagery to the reflections of
objects in the water. Chuang-
Tzu, having dreamt that he was
a butterfly, said, "Who am I in
reality? A butterfly dreaming
that I am Chuang-Tzu, or
Chuang-Tzu dreaming he was a
butterfly?" Kinuko Craft's
modern illustration delicately
portrays the thoughts of both
philosophers.**

Yosl Bergner (1920–),
The Butterfly Eaters   **"All my
paintings are dreams," says
Bergner. As though in a sad
dream, a formally dressed family
sits at a dinner table in the
middle of a dense mire, eating
butterflies (illusions).**

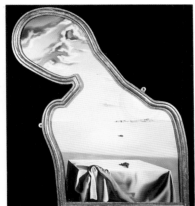

Salvador Dali (1904–1989)
*Couple with their Heads Full of
Clouds* **Fusion and separateness
of Self and Other is a common
theme in dreams. Dreaming of
one's partner often reflects the
dreamer's own self.**

To communicate one's dream is to be in better communication with one's self.

When good things happen I dream of good things; when bad things happen I dream of bad things.

Efrat (a five-year-old girl)

Anonymous, *The Crow People*
Childhood abuse is difficult to recognize in adult dreams. This painted dream by a young woman who had been a childhood victim of incest shows herself as a frail little girl in green (on the left side of the painting). She is approached by frightening elongated figures, and runs to her mother (drawn in profile on the extreme left of the picture), only to discover that the mother herself has turned into one of these terrifying figures. It was through repeated dreams of such nature, and the fragments of associations they produced in therapy, that the woman was able to piece together her past trauma, and to eventually overcome some of its worst effects.

Ilan Kutz (1944–   ), *Tea Cup in a Tempest*   **The sinking of a tea set, the epitome of the ordinary and the stable, creates a feeling of catastrophe. As do images in dreams, those in this painting convey the inner state of affairs.**

Erwin Shenkelbach (1930–)
The Jerusalem Ghost **Life
imitates dreams. While dreams
are imbued with daily scenes,
sometimes a street scene evokes
a dreamy image.**

Giovanni Segantini (1858–1899),
The Punishment of Luxury
Segantini said, "True life is but a dream, the dream of gradually approaching an ideal at once as remote as possible and elevated, elevated to the point that matter vanishes." Segantini was driven higher and higher into isolated alpine peaks in his search for pure light, color, and possibly death.

To understand one's dream is to begin to understand one's self.

Arnold Böcklin (1827–1901),
The Island of the Dead **Böcklin
painted several versions of this
imaginary place of isolation and
retreat from the world, which
haunted him like a repeated
dream. For Böcklin, this
painting, like his others, was "a
picture to make people dream
over."**

Telling the future is being aware of the present.

Entering the Fourth Dimension

In the Fourth Dimension

Returning from the Fourth Dimension

Erwin Shenkelbach (1930–),
The Fourth Dimension (Series)
**As with individual dreams of a
series, each of these dreamlike
photographs stands on its own.
When viewed together, however,
the repetition of images against
a slightly changing background
highlights the common theme of
traversing the edges of reality,
thereby endowing each
individual image with additional
meaning.**

František Kupka (1871–1957), *The Way of Silence* **As in a dream, the tiny figure of Kupka, a devout mystic, faces a row of enigmatic sphinxes, those posers of riddles of the cosmos (represented by the Milky Way) and identity (represented by the hardly legible inscription on the pedestal of the sphinx in the foreground: *"Quam ad Causum Sumus?"*—("Why Are We?").**

A dream created by you is ultimately about you.

René Magritte (1898–1967),
Le Domaine d'Arnheim
Displacement, in dreams and in art, raises doubt about "what seems" and "what is." In this painting, Magritte creates tension through the enigmatic relationship between the eggs in the foreground and the mountain summit, with its eagle-like silhouette.

John Tenniel (1820–1914), *Alice in Wonderland* *"Dear, dear! How queer everything is today! And yesterday things went on just as usual. I wonder if I've been changed in the night? But if I am not the same the next question is, 'Who in the world am I?' Ah,* that's the great *puzzle!"*

"So you think you're changed, do you?" (said the Caterpillar). "I'm afraid I am, Sir," said Alice. "I can't remember things as I used . . . and I don't keep the same size for ten minutes together!"

Lewis Carroll, the author of *Alice's Adventures in Wonderland,* aided by John Tenniel's illustrations, deploys many of the dream's mechanism of displacement, condensation, and distortion of time and place in order to achieve the tale's outlandish, enlightening effects. *Alice in Wonderland* shares with other masterpieces for children of all ages, such as *The Little Prince,* or *Where the Wild Things Are,* the literary device of the dream to enter a world of fantasy, through which are conveyed basic truths about self and identity.

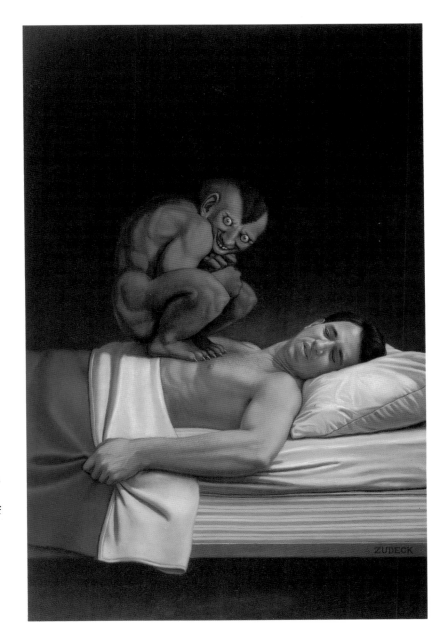

Darryl Zudeck (1961–), *The Nightmare* **This modern version by a New York illustrator, after the original by Yohann Heinrich Fuseli, captures the suffering of the "incubus attack," the tenacious clinging of oppressive evil spirits to the chest of the dreamer. Called "night terrors" today, these terrifying sensations are considered a disturbance of sleep physiology rather than a psychological problem.**

Richard Dadd (1817–1886),
The Fairy Feller's Master Stroke
**Certain dreams portray
themes that haunt the mind.
This eerie painting, like a
dream, conveys
metaphorically the inner
horror of a young, insane
artist who killed his father.**

Sleep is supposed to be,
By souls of sanity,
The shutting of an eye.

Emily Dickinson

Dream interpretation is a game of inner truths. All you have to do is play.

For the starting point seems to be stronger when reason is disengaged.

Aristotle

Ilan Kutz (1944–   ), *The Puzzle*
**In both dreams and paintings,
puzzles of inner landscapes are
created through the use of
fantastic symbols that can be
understood on many levels.**

Yosl Bergner (1920–   ),
The Return of the Wooden Horse
**This dreamlike painting captures
the dread of insecure childhood
in the image of the toy facing a
menacing horizon.**

It seems to me I am trying to tell you a dream—making a vain attempt, because no relation of a dream can convey the dream-sensation, that commingling of absurdity, surprise, and bewilderment in a tremor of struggling revolt, that notion of being captured by the incredible which is of the very essence of dreams.

Joseph Conrad

René Magritte (1898–1967), *The House of Glass* **Magritte liked to think of his paintings as "self-willed dreams, which are not intended to make you sleep, but to wake you up." In this enigmatic portrait, "front" and "back" are condensed, creating a heightened uncertainty and awareness of absurdity.**

I've no Jung to interpret my dreams.

Carl Gustav Jung

Jean Delville (1867–1953),
Soul Love   **Male and female
figures often represent, in
paintings as in dreams, the
spiritual male and female
aspects of the psyche. In
Delville's romantic painting,
these aspects are joined in
harmony. Dreams often portray the
male and female forces in conflict.**

The odd thing about a dream is that while you may not relate to its plot, the plot always relates to you.

Luis Cruz Azaceta (1942–   ),
War Head: Dangerous Dream
**Azaceta, a modern illustrator,
makes use of some of the more
frightening images of modern
devastation. The head, with its
horrified eyes and zipped-up
mouth, unable to talk about the
images of war, mutilation, and
destruction that fill it, conveys
all too vividly an atmosphere of
trauma and post-traumatic
dreams.**

Like the Senoi [a Malaysian jungle tribe], I regard dreaming as indicative of my internal state and take its data into account in my day-to-day self-assessment.

J. Allan Hobson, M.D., Sleep and Dream Researcher

The most skillful interpreter of dreams is he who has the faculty of observing resemblances.

Aristotle

Jerry LoFaro (1959–   ), *The Lay of the Land*   **Archetypal images of sex, fertility, and Mother Earth abound in this contemporary dreamlike journey into an eroticized female landscape.**

Something we were withholding made us weak,
Until we found it was ourselves.

Robert Frost

Gustav Doré (1832–1883),
Job and His Friends   *When I say,
My bed shall comfort me, my couch
shall ease my complaint; Then you
scarest me with dreams, and
terrifiest me through visions: So that
my soul chooseth strangling, and
death rather than life.* (Job 7:13–15)
**Job may have been the first
documented sufferer of post-
traumatic dreams.**

Francis Bacon (1909–   )
"Study from the Human Body"
*This thing of darkness I
acknowledge mine.*" Shakespeare

Ilan Kutz (1944–   ), *Nightbird*
As though in a dream, this haunting and haunted owl, together with the moon in the sky, has become wooden as the tree with which it has merged. Generally a symbol of intuitive wisdom, the owl has been transformed into a personal symbol of wisdom paralyzed.

A dream is too slender a hint to be understood until it is enriched by the stuff of associations and analogy and thus amplified to the point of intelligibility.

Carl Gustav Jung

If a picture is worth a thousand words then a dream is worth a thousand pictures.

René Magritte (1898–1967),
La Condition Humaine **Magritte
blurs the boundary between
painted reality and "reality
itself" (which is another painted
reality), thus making a
statement, as does a dream,
about the inevitable human
uncertainty concerning the
relationship between perception
and actuality.**

The waking have one world in common; sleepers have each a private world of their own.

Heraclitus

In each of us there is another whom we do not know. He speaks to us in dreams and tells us how differently he sees us from the way we see ourselves. When, therefore, we find ourselves in a difficult situation to which there is no solution, he can sometimes kindle a light that radically alters our attitude.

Carl Gustav Jung

Jacob's Ladder   **Jacob's ladder as seen by a twelfth-century artist.**

The dream is a personal myth and myth is a dream of a culture.

Sigmund Freud

Gustav Doré (1832–1883), *Joseph Interpreting Pharaoh's Dream* *And Joseph said unto Pharaoh, The dream of Pharaoh is one: God hath shewed Pharaoh what he is about to do.* (Genesis 41:25).

Joseph's interpretation of the dream of Pharaoh is based on the premise of the divine source of dreams. This is perhaps the first documented interpretation of a series of dreams having one connected meaning.

Hugo Simberg (1875–1917),
The Wounded Angel   **For Hugo
Simberg, a melancholic Finnish
painter, the wounded angel may
have stood for the
unattainability of love or
happiness. But this heart-
wrenching image of the captive,
broken-winged angel, carried as
loot by two peasant boys, can
symbolize the captivity of, or
injury to, the inner self, a theme
so frequent in dreams.**

No man achieves true and inspired divination when in his rational mind, but only when the power of his intelligence is fettered in sleep . . . But it belongs to a man when in his right mind to recollect and ponder both the thing spoken in dream or waking vision . . . and by means of reasoning to discern about them all wherein they are significant.

Plato

Giorgio De Chirico (1888–1978),
The Red Tower **"If a work of art
is to be truly immortal, it must
pass quite beyond the limits of
the human world, without any
sign of common sense and logic.
In this way the work will draw
nearer to the dream."** It was
once said of De Chirico (a
forerunner of the Surrealist
movement) that his paintings
enable the viewer "to see
thought . . . ," a good
description of what dreams do as
well.

Dreams and visions are infused into men for their advantage and instruction.

Artemidorus of Daldis

Yosl Bergner (1920–), *The Alarm*
**Bergner's giant alarm clock, with
its blurred and torn face, looms
over the land. Is it the symbol
for a siren in a country at war? A
metaphor for life's vulnerability?
As with dreams, one is left with
several associations and choices
for interpretation.**

In the business of making meaning from dreams, one has to accept a basic level of ambiguity.

Man's shadow, I thought, is his vanity.

Friedrich Nietzsche

"In the year 1525 between Wednesday and Thursday after Whitsunday, during the night I saw this appearance in my sleep, how many great waters fell from heaven. The first struck the earth about four miles away from me with a terrific force, with tremendous clamor and clash, drowning the whole land. I was so sore afraid that . . . when I awoke, my whole body trembled and for a long time I could not come to myself. So when I arose in the morning, I painted above here as I had seen it. God turn all things to the best."

Albrecht Dürer (1471–1528), *The Deluge* **Dürer's dream occurred at a time of dread stirred by a rumor that a flood would destroy the world. Although Dürer's beautiful painting of his dream may be one of a kind, the premonitory and foreboding content is far from unusual in dreams.**

Yosl Bergner (1920–   ),
The Closet Girl   **Symbols of the
unconscious—here the multiple
image, the reflection in the
water, and the single figure
walking into the dark horizon—
are common in surrealist
paintings and dreams. Bergner's
painting evokes existential issues
of identity, constant uncertainty,
and anxiety.**

Henri Rousseau (1844–1910), *La Charmeuse de Serpents* ("The Snake Charmer") **A customs official and self-taught painter, Henri Rousseau is known for his creation of bizarre, symbolic paintings, much like dreams. In this painting, the shadow-figure, the snakes, the moon, the water, and the lush vegetation are all archetypes that occupy the inner landscape of the unconscious.**

S	M	T	W	T	F	S

MONTH:_____ YEAR:_____

S	M	T	W	T	F	S

MONTH: _____ *YEAR:* _____

S	M	T	W	T	F	S

MONTH: _____ *YEAR:* _____

S	M	T	W	T	F	S

MONTH: _____ *YEAR:* _____

S	M	T	W	T	F	S

MONTH: _____ *YEAR:* _____

S	M	T	W	T	F	S

*MONTH:*_____ *YEAR:*_____

S	M	T	W	T	F	S

MONTH: _____ YEAR: _____

S	M	T	W	T	F	S

MONTH:_____ YEAR:_____

S	M	T	W	T	F	S

MONTH:_____ YEAR:_____

S	M	T	W	T	F	S

MONTH: _____ *YEAR:* _____

S	M	T	W	T	F	S

MONTH:_____ YEAR:_____

S	M	T	W	T	F	S

MONTH: _____ YEAR: _____

RECOMMENDED READING LIST

1. J. Allan Hobson: *Sleep.* **Scientific American Library. 1989.**
A most comprehensive, informative, up-to-date, and delightfully illustrated book that tells you everything you wanted to know about the phenomenon of sleep, its origin, structure, disturbances, and more. It includes a review of the physiology of dreaming. A must.

2. J. Allan Hobson: *The Dreaming Brain.* **Basic Books. 1988.**
An in-depth journey into the physiology of sleep and dreaming, with special emphasis on the activation synthesis theory of dreaming.

3. Ernest Hartmann: *The Nightmare.* **Basic Books. 1984.**
A broad overview of the psychology and biology of nightmares, and of those who suffer from them.